FROM THE GAVEL TO GRACE

SETTING PEOPLE FREE FROM ADDICTION AND INTO HEALING

BRETT KNIGHT

DEDICATION

This book is dedicated to all of those battling on the front lines of the war against addiction. May this book serve as a weapon, a tool, and an encouragement.

"For though we walk in the flesh, we do not war according to the flesh. For the weapons of our warfare are not carnal but mighty in God for pulling down strongholds, casting down arguments and every high thing that exalts itself against the knowledge of God, bringing every thought into captivity to the obedience of Christ..." (2 Cor 10:3–5 NKJV)

"The Spirit of the Lord is upon Me,

Because He has anointed Me

To preach the gospel to the poor;

He has sent Me to heal the brokenhearted,

To proclaim liberty to the captives

And recovery of sight to the blind,

To set at liberty those who are oppressed;"

(Luke 4:18 NKJV)

TABLE OF CONTENTS

INTRODUCTION

There's a stack of laminated obituaries in my conference room. I keep them there for a reason, and I look at them often. Each obituary in the pile is a familiar face, a client whose name I knew and whose life I prayed for.

I fought hard for these brothers and sisters. I did my best to help them break free from addiction. Some I represented in court. Some I baptized. Some I buried. And some I did all three. I was in the fight with them when addiction claimed them.

I don't keep these obituaries as some kind of morbid decoration. I keep them to remind myself of the all-out war we're fighting against addiction in our country. This is not a game, and it's not a drill. I'm not going to sugarcoat it. If we lose, the result isn't just relapse—it's death.

That's why when someone walks into my office with fresh track marks on their arms or bloodshot eyes, I don't judge them. I fight next to them. I've seen too many coffins and stood in front of too many grieving families with the Bible in one hand and the other fist clenched in anger.

And every time, I find myself asking God, "Why couldn't we save this one?"

Those laminated pieces of paper are reminders of my daily convictions. Somewhere between the courtroom and the church pew, I learned the hard way that you can't punish the pain out of people. You can only love them to freedom.

I used to believe the courtroom was where change happened. I thought that if we made the consequences harsh enough, people would finally turn their lives around. Then I saw firsthand how punishment never healed anyone. It often pushed them further away from hope and straight back into the arms of addiction. Through it all, I've found a balance between the gavel and grace, and I believe living in that balance is the path to hope and freedom.

But I can't walk that path alone. There are too many people who need help. The impact of addiction is too widespread. That's why this book exists.

I wrote this book to be a manual for chain breakers willing to stand in the gap for those who can't make sound judgments for themselves.

I wrote it to support families clinging to their last shred of hope, desperate to understand the loved ones they're losing to addiction.

I wrote it for judges, prosecutors, and defense attorneys who feel trapped in a revolving system that punishes pain but doesn't seem to heal it.

And I wrote it for churches and communities who are willing to open their doors wider to the people most of society has written off.

The truth is, addiction isn't a moral failure. Addiction is most often the result of unhealed pain, and justice without grace doesn't restore—it breaks. When I got tired of watching it break people over and over again, I was left with just one question:

> What happens when grace and mercy walk into the courtroom?

That's the question that changed my life. The answer? Well, the answer will change *yours*.

"God, Show Me What I'm Missing"

I've had a lot of success in my life, but I have learned that success can't protect you from pain. I was in my mid-20s when my brother died in a car accident at age 29. It shattered me. My faith, which had been mostly intellectual up to that point, fell apart. I decided I'd rather numb the pain than face it. Instead of turning to drugs or alcohol, I became addicted to work and the pursuit of success.

I spent almost 20 years in the corporate world before I went to law school. When I graduated and got hired as an assistant district attorney, I honestly believed that if I helped the system punish people enough, they'd change. That's how I planned to make a difference—by punishing the addiction right out of them and right out of my community. As an assistant district attorney, I had the power and the right to prosecute to the full extent of the law.

The problem was, it didn't work. It didn't take long for me to realize that the punishments I was handing out weren't helping shrink the drug problem. For every person I sent to prison, two more showed up to take their place. And the people I put in prison went right back to addiction the moment they were on the other side of the bars.

I started to feel like the boy with his finger in the dam trying to hold back an entire river. As long as people had a desire for drugs, someone, usually a local drug user, would step in and take over their clientele to pay for their own habit. Every person I put in jail created the opportunity for someone else to become a dealer. It seemed like the only thing I was doing was getting people promoted from user to dealer.

One night, in frustration, I prayed: "God, show me what I'm missing. Show me what You know that I don't. Let me see what you see."

That prayer changed everything. Immediately, my perspective shifted, and I began to see addicts differently. Instead of seeing them as criminals who needed to be punished, I began seeing them as someone's son or daughter. I realized each one was a person whose choices were often born out of pain and trauma they didn't know how to escape. I began seeing the person as clearly as I saw the trauma.

Once I saw it, I couldn't unsee it. It was like a light bulb went on. I realized that as long as these men and women were stuck in pain and trauma, another prison sentence wouldn't redeem them. Punishment wasn't doing a thing to help them heal. They might come out of the system clean, but they'd be thrown back into the same pain and trauma that caused them to turn to drugs in the first place.

Suddenly, all I could see at sentencing hearings was what prison without healing meant for them. The young man who walked into his hearing wearing his own polo and blue jeans? That would be the last time he'd wear his own clothes for years. The woman who'd shared her love of chocolate milkshakes with me just two days ago? Who knew when the next time she'd have a chance to order her own food would be?

Those are small things, but just as prison changes a person's life in the here and now, it also affects their future. Some prisoners never come home, and those who do end up with a label that follows them, affecting where they can live and work.

Addiction can be its own prison too. A cell isn't always made of physical bars. Some cells are made of pain and shame. If we don't reach people fast enough, that cell hardens, keeping them trapped in addiction.

Maybe it's time to start breaking chains instead of forging new ones.

What You'll Learn in This Book

This book is not a memoir. This book is a field manual for chain breakers like me who want to see people set free *and* healed. I'll tell you more about my path from poor kid to pastor in the next chapter. Along the way, you'll hear how I became a criminal defense attorney and how the courtroom became my mission field.

The real story behind this book began in the courtroom, when I realized that grace can do what the gavel was never meant to do. People need someone to believe that they are still worth saving. They need hope. They need help healing from their pain and trauma so they can get clean and stay clean.

The methods we're using in the courtroom now aren't helping as much as they need to, and we've tried everything. We've tried punishment. We've tried shame. We've tried looking away. None of that works because none of it heals. You can't punish pain away. In this book, you're going to learn what *does* work.

In part 1, I'll outline the problem we're facing. The current approach keeps recycling the same outcomes by criminalizing pain. Instead of healing the causes of addiction, we punish symptoms. You'll see how the "perception gap" distorts decisions in courtrooms and families. Then I'll show you my five-step formula that helps families walk their loved ones through navigating the justice system in a way that helps the addicted individual get *real* help.

In part 2, you'll learn about the root cause of addiction. Addiction often stems from unhealed pain, trauma, identity loss, and spiritual fracture. You'll learn how to respond with compassion and accountability without enabling or allowing your boundaries to be walked on.

In part 3, we'll shed some light on what happens between the gavel and grace. I'll show you what treatment-forward justice looks like in real life with furloughs, structured programs, and review hearings. I've helped hundreds break free from addiction with these methods, and I can't wait to share them— and true stories of people whose lives have been impacted— with you.

In part 4, I'll dive into the ripple effect that one changed life can cause. You'll learn simple models for restoring families and communities through partnerships with local groups and organizations. Support is the key that turns isolated wins into community transformation and momentum.

Finally, in part 5, I'll show you how you can stand in the gap and become part of the solution. Whether you're a parent, a judge or attorney, a pastor, or a community leader, you can make a difference. There's also a whole chapter with insights for parents that will help you break the cycle of addiction so future generations don't struggle.

Who This Book Is For

This book is for families. This book will teach you how to respond in a crisis without enabling and what to say when you don't know what to say. You'll learn where to start with treatment options, support groups, and how to build a "circle of care." I'll also give you my 5-step formula for how to work with courts, probation, attorneys, community organizations, treatment centers, and churches to pursue treatment-forward paths.

This book is for legal professionals, court advocates, probation officers, and recovery advocates. You'll learn practical alternatives to punishment alone, including agreements, reviews, and accountability tools that can help defendants get the help they need and reintegrate into society. I'll show you how to spot when a defendant's issue is unhealed trauma and what to ask. You'll also learn courtroom language that builds compliance, not resistance.

This book is for churches and community leaders. You'll learn how to open your doors safely and wisely and how to run family and community nights that create "contagious hope." I'll also share discipleship frameworks for people in early recovery that provide mercy and structure.

Hope spreads. And when it does, things can change fast. I've seen hope spread during family nights and in church basements. I've watched the Holy Spirit meet people the moment they cracked open the door of their hearts. Grace does what punishment never could. Finding ways to help people break the chains of addiction is my calling; I hope that as you read this book, the same can become part of your calling too.

I didn't set out to stand between justice and the broken. I started on one side of that line, believing that punishment would fix what pain had broken. It took years in courtrooms and even longer in my own life to learn that mercy and accountability aren't opposites. They're actually partners, and I've seen what happens when we choose one without the other. In chapter 1, I'll share how I went from poverty to prosecutor, only to find that what I thought would help instead contributed to the rise of addiction.

PART 1

THE PROBLEM

You Can't Punish Pain Away

"The spirit of a man will sustain him in sickness, But who can bear a broken spirit?" (Prov 18:14 NKJV)

From Poverty to Prosecutor

Before my life was ever touched by addiction, and before I ever stood in a courtroom or wore a suit, I was just a kid growing up in poverty in Southern Illinois.

My parents loved us, but when I say we were poor, I mean we were *poor*. Not only was money tight, but it was challenging for my parents to keep my brothers and me fed and with clothes on our backs. The walls of our house were bare studs with insulation in between. No drywall. There were years we didn't have running water. In the winter, we often woke up with frost on the inside of the windows. I can still remember sleeping under eight blankets in the middle of winter because the only heat in the house was the kitchen stove. Even now, when I lie down and close my eyes on a cold winter night, I can still feel the weight of those blankets.

So yeah, I was the kid who showed up to school wearing ripped jeans and dirty clothes. That's all I had. Despite our poverty, I was happy, and if you asked me what kind of childhood I had, I'd tell you I had a good one. My parents were far from perfect. They liked to drink and had regular get-togethers with

75 to 100 people. Someone would show up with a guitar, then another, and someone had a drum set they could bring over. My father would hold court all day at a barbecue grill made from an old oil drum while he cooked half a deer over hot coals. He would stand there at that grill with a small towel hanging out of his back pocket while men, young and old, gathered around him. Man, did he love telling stories of hunting trips long ago. I credit my father with my social skills. I would watch in awe as he held a crowd captive with his words and personality.

My mother was the hostess. Contrary to my father, she never stood still. She was always running in and out of the house to get another Tupperware bowl of potato salad or hug the most recent addition to the growing crowd. I'm like my mom in that way too; I can't sit still. If you see me at events, even church, you'll notice I'm always moving around. You will often find me walking around to the back of the sanctuary during worship music to greet people coming in a little late and give them a hug. (Yes, I'm a hugger, just like she was.)

To set the record straight, we never actually had Tupperware. We used empty butter containers that we affectionately called Tupperware. We learned the hard way to never try to microwave leftover chili in one though. When I look back, picturing that scene in my mind makes me smile. To this day, when I see old friends I grew up with, we reminisce about those years growing up at the city lake. Inevitably, we end up laughing about something that happened at one of those get-togethers. But the thing I remember the most is that they loved us and took care of us to the best of their ability.

My mom worked in what I can best describe as a biker bar, so I grew up with 15 "uncles" in leather vests. I didn't realize it until I was a teenager, but there were years when she put almost as much cocaine across the bar as she did beer. A normal Friday night for me was hanging out at the local arcade. When all the other kids went home, I'd walk down to the bar and sit at the end of the big wooden counter, drinking a Coke. I talked and laughed with the people there until Mom closed the place and took me home. To me, it was completely normal to bring your prom date to the bar so your mom could see the dress.

Somehow, by the grace of God, beyond the occasional recreational use of marijuana as a young man, I never got into drugs. I worked hard in school, but probably not as hard as I should have. It became obvious to everyone early on that I had a speech impediment. There were many sounds, words, and combinations of letters that I could not say correctly. The school had a special speech program, and for many years, I would be taken out of the regular class to get help with my speech. That little delay at a young age caused me to doubt myself as I grew up. I believe it was that doubt, along with the home environment I grew up in, that caused me to be less of a young scholar than perhaps I should have been.

Education was not a priority in my home. My father quit school in ninth grade, and my mother only made it through tenth. There was not a single example of someone who graduated high school in my family, never mind going on to college. It just wasn't anything that was discussed in our house. We talked about work and about being the kind of person who could be trusted, but we never discussed education.

While academics may have been low on my priority list, I was active in many things at school. I loved theater and took theater classes all four years of high school, finding that speaking in front of audiences helped me overcome my speech impediment. I enjoyed history and government classes, was in many extracurricular activities and clubs, and excelled at everything I was interested in. There were certain things I was excluded from because I just couldn't afford much, but I made friends easily and was well-liked. I was even elected class president in high school and served on the student council.

Looking back, student council was where I discovered that there was more potential inside me than I'd realized. My eighth grade government teacher, a man named George Hopkins, saw something in me that no one else seemed to see, including myself. He pulled me aside one day after class and told me he would like me to run for student council.

"Why?" I asked. I had never given something like that a single thought.

"There is something about you that the other kids are drawn to," he replied kindly. "You're a natural leader."

A natural leader? Me? I had no idea what he was talking about, but for the next few days, I could not get his suggestion out of my head. With one two-minute conversation, Mr. Hopkins nudged my future in a positive direction because he cared about all of his students, including me. He wanted to impact our lives, and he sure impacted mine.

At Mr. Hopkins' suggestion, I ran for student council. To my surprise, my classmates elected me! Even after 40 years, I can still remember the look on my mom's face when I told her. Genuine and unconcealed pride shone from her eyes. As adults, we greatly underestimate the power we have to plant seeds in the minds of young people. Seeds are cheap and easy to plant, but they can produce abundant crops. Never underestimate the power of planting positive seeds.

Not everyone was as encouraging as Mr. Hopkins. Despite my growth and accomplishments, the message I heard from most of the world was clear: *Stay where you belong.* I'll never forget walking into my high school guidance counselor's office for one of those "it's time to get ready for your future" meetings that every student had to have.

"Hey Brett," he said, waving me into his office. He shuffled some papers around on his desk until he pulled out a plain manila folder with my name on the side. "Have a seat."

I sat down in the uncomfortable chair across the desk from him as he skimmed the contents of the folder. It didn't take long. Then he shut the folder, pushed it off to the side of his desk, and looked me right in the eye.

"Well, Brett, not everybody's meant to go to college. You either need to get a vocational career or join the military."

Message received. In less than ten minutes, I walked out of his office that day knowing that he thought I'd never amount to much. I wasn't angry with him, but it set me back. It spoke to the place in the back of my mind that said, "You're just a poor kid from a rundown house. You'll never be anything special." Again, seeds are powerful, for good *and* for bad. Eventually, his words would light a fire in me to prove him wrong. It just took me a little while to get there.

Ten days after high school graduation, I found myself in basic training after joining the Navy. I turned 18 while in basic training. Happy birthday to me. I spent three of my last ten days before basic training on in-house suspension at my high school. Yes, I spent three days on in-house suspension AFTER I graduated. Let's just say I was a bit of a cut up, and the idea of setting a pig loose in the second-floor hallway of the school seemed like a reasonable thing at the time. We will move on from that story, as I am not sure what the statute of limitations is on high school pranks in Illinois.

Later on, I got a job doing television repair and satellite installations. I went on to work at a Christian television station, then I took a job doing construction work for a family friend. I stuck with these jobs for about five years. During one hot roof removal job in July, I decided college didn't sound too bad. Later that fall, I walked onto campus at Southern Illinois University (SIU) as a freshman.

I wasn't your typical college freshman. Most students see college as a place to finally be on their own, spread their wings, and have some fun. But by that time, I had a young child at home, and I tackled college like a timed exam. I loaded myself with classes and set myself on a path to graduate in three years.

It was while I was at SIU that a political science professor named Dr. Ron Mason saw something in me. Dr. Mason reminded me so much of Mr. Hopkins because they both were tall, thin, athletic men who had played professional baseball and taught government. Looking back, I marvel at how God makes a way for us. At another crossroad, a familiar kind of man appeared in my life and pointed out my potential. God knew I wouldn't listen to just anyone, so He put someone with a familiar personality and features in my path. God cared so much for me and truly meant it when He said in the book of Jeremiah, "For I know the thoughts that I think toward you, says the Lord, thoughts of peace and not of evil, to give you a future and a hope." (Jer 29:11 NIV)

Out of a crowd of more than 100 students, Dr. Mason also saw something in me. It's like the God of the universe took the time to put someone in my life to give me another positive nudge. I didn't know it yet, but that is exactly what I was about to get—a future and a hope.

Dr. Mason started challenging me with questions and discussions after class. Halfway through the first semester, he invited me to lunch. Dr. Mason took me under his wing and mentored me, eventually making me his research assistant. I ended up changing my major to political science, and I soaked up every bit of instruction Dr. Mason gave me. He taught me how leadership, decision-making, and morality intersect. He also taught me that a person could use their brain, not just their back, to make money.

I didn't realize it at the time, but now I can see that he was testing me—no, *daring* me—to be the person I was capable of being. We discussed class topics some, but most of the time we discussed scholarly articles and books by authors that he recommended to me. We started with Thomas Paine, Jean-Jacques Rousseau, and John Stuart Mill. Then we moved on to

Thomas Hobbes, Niccolò Machiavelli, Milton Friedman, and F.A. Hayek.

The conversation always revolved around a central theme: "What is the most effective and efficient way a group of people can decide issues?" Dr. Mason would purposefully bait me into a debate, then set the logical trap. I worked hard to anticipate where the flaws in my argument might be and shore them up. It was a wonderful time in my life, and there's not much I wouldn't do to have a few more of those conversations.

During my last year at SIU, Dr. Mason hired me to write training materials for his consulting firm on how to make group decisions. When one of my coworkers got injured, I stepped in and delivered the training on his behalf, even though I'd never done anything like that before.

At the end of the project, Dr. Mason handed me an envelope and said, "Here, you earned it." When I looked inside, I couldn't believe it. He'd given me $5,000—his entire commission for the project. I'd never seen so much money in one place before. That moment changed everything. It gave me a taste of success, and I wanted more.

Addicted to Success

When I graduated from college, I had three opportunities in front of me. One, I was offered a permanent position in my professor's consulting firm. Two, I was asked to join the staff of a state senator I'd volunteered with during my college years. And last, I was given the opportunity to stay at SIU as a student teacher and attend law school for free. I had to resist the urge to send a letter with a copy of my transcript and good grades to my high school guidance counselor with a note saying, "Not everyone is meant to be a guidance counselor. Perhaps you should consider a vocational career or join the military."

I was intrigued by the idea of going to law school. It was definitely something I wanted to do, but as a young married man with a child and a new baby at home, I went with the only option that made sense at the time. I took the consulting job, and I did it well.

I began traveling all over the country, making more money than anyone I knew growing up ever had. While I was on the road, I became a voracious reader. I was convinced that if I could learn it, I could do it, so I read two to three books per week. I read about communication, leadership, business, personal development, growth—you name it. I read about it, then I put it into action.

I built a solid career, earning impressive titles and the salary to go along with it. And I became addicted to that success. My drug wasn't a substance. It was the look of admiration and awe on people's faces when they learned what I'd come from and what I'd accomplished. So what if I was gone most of the time?

But my wife didn't see it that way, and I couldn't understand why. I didn't cheat, and she had everything she could ever ask for. What more did she want? Well, for one thing, she needed my time. All the success came at a steep cost. I lost my marriage, my family, and my faith.

I'd become a Christian years before, but I had approached it like I did everything else—by reading everything I could about it. I learned the Bible backward and forward and dove into studying the original Greek and Hebrew, consulting concordances, and more…but the knowledge never got much farther than my head. When all you have is head knowledge, at the first bump in the road, your faith will fall out of your ears. That's what happened to me. I decided to just do my own thing. I didn't have much to do with God.

For a while, things were okay. But when my brother died in a car accident at age 29, the pain broke me. He and I had been very close, and I was forced to stop and take a hard look at my life. Within a year's time, I had lost my brother and best friend and was newly divorced. Other than work, I didn't have a life. I was ready to stop living on the road and put down some roots.

So I got out a map. I wanted somewhere that was big enough to offer the kind of professional opportunities I was looking for, but close enough that I could still see my kids often and visit my parents easily. I narrowed it down to three cities—St. Louis, Indianapolis, and Nashville. In the end, I chose Nashville. I'd been there before, and I'd always liked it. Without much of a plan besides a destination on a map, I quit my job, packed up my stuff, and moved.

I didn't know a soul in Nashville, but a friend of a friend connected me with someone who had part of a house for rent. With a place to lay my head, I started pounding the pavement for a job. Within days, I landed an IT position that eventually resulted in my being hired at a Brazilian aircraft manufacturer, where I worked for a number of years.

It was a great job, but I couldn't stop thinking about becoming a lawyer. It had been years since the seed had been planted, but I had never forgotten it.

I stayed with the airline company, eventually becoming head of the IT department for the Nashville location. Working in IT was great. It satisfied my desire to constantly learn and grow, and it was financially rewarding as well. But I still couldn't stop thinking about becoming a lawyer. I went on to work as a director at a document management company, where I designed computer systems for companies all over the Southeast. Even then, the idea of law school was in the back of my mind. It was during this time that I met an amazing woman named Donna, and we got married.

I'm not afraid to dive in and apply myself to something new, but I *am* afraid of living with regrets. I credit my wife, Donna, in large part for my success. From the time I met and married her, I have never known a more supportive person. I could come up with some crazy, risky idea, and she would just listen and say, "I think you can make it work." When I came to her and said, "I want to go to law school," her response was, "You would be great at that."

I don't know too many people who would encourage their spouse to leave behind a good-paying career to chase after a dream, but my wife did. Just like the power of a seed planted, don't ever underestimate the value of having someone who supports you wholeheartedly. I would not have made it through law school, gone into private practice, become a pastor, or written this book if she had not encouraged me and stood beside me all the way.

So once again, with the support of my family, I jumped into the deep end of the pool. I quit my job and enrolled in law school at Belmont University. Because of my background in technology, I managed to land a sought-after internship with the district attorney general (DA), a man named Randy York. Getting an internship with the district attorney is not easy, but I was willing to be creative.

I followed community events and tried to guess which ones the DA would attend. I would then go to these local events and make sure I introduced myself to Randy. I know at one point I told Donna that I was either going to get this internship or get arrested for stalking. One evening, at a swearing-in ceremony, I happened to (on purpose) leave at the same time as Randy. We were alone in the elevator, and he turned to me and said, "Okay, we have about two minutes until we get to the first floor. Why should I hire you?"

I gave the pitch of my life in that elevator, and I was in! The internship began just a few months later. Part of my responsibilities included working closely with the drug task force, helping them utilize wiretapping and surveillance within the boundaries of the law. I received a special license that allowed me to practice law even as I finished my last year and a half of law school. I spent more time at the DA's office working these cases than I did in the law library, but the gamble paid off. When I graduated with my law degree, they hired me full-time as an assistant district attorney.

What It Looks Like Out There

When I stepped into the courtroom as part of the drug task force handling various criminal cases, I expected to find justice. What I actually found was a front-row seat to the American drug crisis.

It should come as no surprise to anyone that the American drug crisis isn't confined to back alleys or big cities anymore. It's in every zip code, every income level, and every school district. I've watched it destroy families that once looked picture-perfect on Sunday mornings. I've watched it grind down men who once held good jobs and women who once drove carpools and taught Bible school.

I'm convinced that underneath the drug problem in America— the root cause of most of it—is a layer of pain, and the justice system has criminalized it.

Almost every addict I've ever met (and I've worked with thousands) was trying to survive something. Some form of trauma, loss, or loneliness was causing them to reach for a needle, a bottle, or a pill to try to ease the pain. Instead of freedom, they ended up with physical, emotional, and spiritual bondage.

In 2024, the United States saw an estimated 80,391 drug overdose deaths. Although that number is down from more than 110,000 the year before, it's still one of the highest totals in history.[1] Even with that decline, overdose death rates remain

---

[1] Centers for Disease Control and Prevention, "U.S. Overdose Deaths Decrease Almost 27% in 2024," news release, May 14, 2025, https://www.cdc.gov.

near record highs, hovering around 31 deaths per 100,000 people nationwide.[2]

Behind those statistics are human faces. Each number represents a son, daughter, father, mother, sister, or brother who was breathing one day and gone the next.

The rise of synthetic opioids, like fentanyl, has changed everything. Personally, I'm convinced fentanyl is a weapon of mass destruction disguised as a drug. It's cheap, it's everywhere, and it's mixed into everything. More often than not, when I review a client's drug screen as their criminal defense attorney, fentanyl shows up in their systems. Many times, my clients are shocked. They *thought* they bought something else but had unknowingly been sold fentanyl instead. Why?

Drug manufacturers use fentanyl to increase their profits. A very high percentage of pills sold on the street today are made in pill presses, not obtained from pharmacies. Illegal drug manufacturers use fentanyl, then label it as other drugs. Fentanyl is cheaper to get, so dealers make more money off of it. Same for heroin or methamphetamine.

The worst part is, the rise of fentanyl has led to an increasing number of overdoses.[3] Fentanyl is 50 to 100 times more potent than many opioids.[4] If a user believes they are buying

---

[2] Matthew F. Garnett and Arialdi M. Miniño, "Drug Overdose Deaths in the United States, 2023–2024," *NCHS Data Brief*, no. 549 (Hyattsville, MD: National Center for Health Statistics, 2026), https://www.cdc.gov/nchs/data/databriefs/db549.pdf.

[3] Centers for Disease Control and Prevention, "U.S. Overdose Deaths Decrease Almost 27% in 2024," news release, May 14, 2025, https://www.cdc.gov.

[4] Centers for Disease Control and Prevention, "Fentanyl," CDC Injury Center, accessed March 5, 2026, https://www.cdc.gov/stopoverdose/fentanyl/index.html.

OxyContin but ends up with fentanyl, they'll dose far too high. You see the problem, right? We must act now. What's on the streets today is so much more powerful and dangerous than anything on the streets even five years ago. We are seeing first-time users overdose. Even people who have used substances for decades have died from these powerful cocktails pressed into pills.

According to the National Institute on Drug Abuse, more than 9 million Americans misuse opioids each year, and nearly 5.7 million live with an opioid use disorder.[5] The only reason we're not stacking bodies in the streets is because of Narcan, a nasal spray that can reverse an overdose in seconds. Yet even that is just a Band-Aid on a gaping wound.

The part that keeps me up at night is that most people experiencing drug addiction who end up in the justice system never get help. It's not because they don't want it, but because the justice system isn't built to heal. It's built to push people through.

On any given day, I've seen dockets packed with 100 to 150 cases. Human lives are reduced to file numbers, and all around them are prosecutors and defense attorneys negotiating settlements and judges approving them. Everyone's under pressure to move cases forward. They often can't take the time to dig deeper. In fact, an overwhelming majority of cases of all people convicted in Tennessee, where I live, end in negotiated

---

[5] National Institute on Drug Abuse, *NIDA HEAL Opioid Use Disorder and Overdose Strategic Plan FY 2025–2029*(Bethesda, MD: National Institutes of Health, 2025), https://nida.nih.gov/publications/nidaheal-opioid-use-disorder-overdose-strategic-plan-fy-2025-2029.

settlements, AKA plea deals.[6] That means people aren't getting trials. They're getting *processed*. Given the volume of cases in the system today, these negotiated settlements are essential to keep the courts from collapsing under the weight.

Once a sentence is handed down, the clock resets.

First offense, probation.

Second offense, some jail time and longer, stricter probation.

Third offense, just go to prison.

Once someone is sent to prison, they serve their time until they are released. By the time they get out, they've lost their job, their home, their family—and they still haven't addressed the pain that started it all. They're pushed back into the community, where they quickly fall back into old crowds and old habits. They relapse, get re-arrested, and the cycle continues.

We're punishing symptoms—pain—instead of healing what's causing them. That's not justice. That's recycling despair.

Now, I get it. It's easy to mistake movement for progress. But just because cases are being checked off doesn't mean lives are changing. Families are collapsing outside the courtroom while inside, we congratulate ourselves on "clearing the docket."

It was in the middle of all that motion of moving one broken life after another through the system that I began to see what justice without grace and mercy really looks like, which changed everything for me.

---

[6] Tennessee Administrative Office of the Courts, *Tennessee Judicial Branch Annual Report* (Nashville: Tennessee Courts, various years), https://www.tncourts.gov

When Justice Meets the Broken

It's one thing to talk about justice in theory, and another to stare it in the face while a mother weeps at your conference table.

Her name was Susan*. By the time she walked into my conference room, she was exhausted. Her son, Kyle*, had been arrested again. It wasn't his first time, and at this rate, it probably wasn't going to be his last. She'd already bonded him out more times than she could count. Each time she hoped things would be different, but a few weeks or months later, she'd be watching him slide right back into the same darkness. This is her story.

* Names changed to protect the privacy of the individual.

Susan's Story

The first time I found out Kyle was using drugs, it was heroin. I've heard people say you feel like you've been kicked in the stomach, but until I experienced it, I had no idea what that felt like. I couldn't breathe. This couldn't be true, but it was.

Once I'd had a chance for it to sink in, I felt like the worst mom. How could I have raised a kid on drugs? Kyle was a good kid. He had parents who were very involved. We love him. We never did anything like drugs in our lives. We didn't even drink alcohol. How could we have a son on drugs? When they say you'd better humble yourself before God has to do it, they are not kidding, because it definitely hurts when God humbles you.

So the next move is to fix him. I mean, as his mom, that's my job, right? That's what moms do. They fix things. But what I learned is I can't fix Kyle...but I sure tried. Some of the things I tried included snooping on his phone. I searched out the people he was hanging around with. I searched his room. I bought drug tests, and I was going to test him if he even walked funny. I followed him around to see if I could catch him using drugs. I even forced him into rehab not once, but twice. It didn't work. Nothing I could do could make him stop using drugs.

What I couldn't understand was that while we're not rich, he came from a decent home. He had a clean home, food to eat, running water, and electricity. Yet he would rather live in a trap house with other addicts doing his drugs than in a decent home without his drugs.

Trying to save him became my second job. I can remember being out at 2 a.m., driving around looking for him. No one even knew I was out. If I had a wreck, if anything had happened to me, no one would've even known. I would just wake up, scared that he wasn't okay. I'd try to call him, and after no answer, I'd just get in my car and go looking. I called all of his friends, messaging them on Facebook to ask if they had seen him, but of course, no one did. So I became the mom out in the middle of the night, knocking on doors asking, "Have you seen Kyle?"

All of this took a toll on me. My anxiety was out of control. I ended up being put on medication for it. This went on for over ten years, and as he got worse, I got worse. It's funny because most moms of boys will blame the girls they're dating, but I have to say, Kyle always dated wonderful girls. No one influenced him. Kyle, when he was clean, dated girls who approved of his lifestyle. And when he began to use drugs, he dated girls who approved of that lifestyle too. Kyle chose this life for himself.

The shame I felt was unbearable at times. I would come home from work, lock my doors, turn off my phone, and just cry. I didn't want to talk to anyone, and I felt so alone because I couldn't help him. How can a mom not help their child? But I couldn't, and I couldn't deal with people's judgment. They looked at him like he was trash, but I saw so much more. Even family members wanted nothing to do with him.

Everyone had suggestions on how I needed to handle this situation. I just needed to walk away. I needed to kick him out. I needed to do the tough love thing, but none of them were handling anything like what I was dealing with. I had a son on drugs, and no one I could talk to. There was no one who could understand how I felt as his mother. This was my child. Everyone wanted me to throw him out to cut him off, but I couldn't do it. My home became my safe place where I could just cry out to God and beg Him to help my son.

For whatever reason, the first time Kyle was arrested, someone called me and said, "I just saw him pulled over and they got handcuffs on him." My heart sank. Don't ask me why, because I still don't know, but for whatever reason, I jumped in my car. I had to go see. As I pulled up, he was still there in handcuffs in the back of the police car. I remember walking up to the police and asking, "Did you find the drugs? Did you find drugs? Is he going to jail?"

They just said, "Ma'am, we can't answer that. We can't give you any information on him."

I said, "Please look again. Search the truck. Call the dogs. Do whatever you have to do, but you have to find drugs on him."

He calmed me and said, "Ma'am, we found drugs. He is going to be arrested."

I just kept saying, "Thank you!" and the officer looked at me so strangely.

"Most times, moms are here to beg us not to take their child, and you're crying, begging us to search his truck for drugs?" he said. "I don't understand." He looked at me and said, "I told him when I put the cuffs on him that he didn't belong here. I could tell that."

I was so proud in that moment. Someone could see what I did. He could see this wasn't who Kyle was. I remember telling him, "Now I can make him go to rehab. I'm gonna make him get help." And I did.

When he came home, he looked so good. I was so proud. But within two days, Kyle overdosed and spent time in the hospital. How does someone go from rehab to an overdose? I still don't understand that, but from hospital door to rehab door, he went back. This time, he went to Cumberland Heights, one of the best rehab centers around.

He was there for three weeks, and then did outpatient for 12 weeks. For a short time, Kyle looked good. It's funny, but if he was doing okay, it was like I could breathe for a short period of time. But in no time, he would be back using drugs again. I remember one of the most hurtful things he ever said to me. I commented on how good he had been doing, and he looked at me and said, "Funny you should say that, because I've been using drugs for about the past month. Even you know I'm better on drugs."

That crushed me. Why would he ever think he was a better person on drugs?

So I have completely given my life up to chase after and try to save my son from addiction. I have no friends. I have no life. I have nothing because I have no time for anything. All my time is devoted to him.

I think there comes a point at which you will try anything, and so I signed myself up for Parents of Prodigals. It's a group of parents who are going through the same thing. It's funny because you should feel safe around others whose kids are struggling with addiction, but the truth is you don't. Or at least I didn't. The place I felt the most safe was when I went to Alcoholics Anonymous (AA) meetings. I remember asking them, "How do I save my son?"

And as I would sit with other drug addicts, I would take in everything they would tell me. I was willing to try anything. I would always ask Kyle to go, and of course, he always had a reason why he wouldn't. AA was a crock, according to him, and it would never work for him. All I knew was I wanted as much information about addiction as I could get. I went to seminars. I searched online for parents who had a child on drugs and would listen to their stories of how their child had gotten into recovery, so I could learn how they helped get their kids clean.

Of course, the answer was I couldn't do anything. It had to be his decision to get clean and stay clean. One thing I did know was that if Kyle was gonna get clean, it was gonna take the mighty hand of God to get a hold of him.

The shame parents feel is real. We are judged by how well our kids turn out, and if they are an addict, then according to society, you failed as a parent. You get the looks of "Bless her heart, her son is on drugs." And while you are so mad at your child, you can't stand for anyone to say anything bad about your child. It's like that whole sibling thing. You can think badly about your sibling, but no one else had better say anything bad about them.

I think it's harder on mothers because God created us to be nurturing and the caregivers of the family. My husband could do the tough love, but I couldn't, and that caused issues in our marriage. That's another area that can really take a toll. Especially when you have different ideas on how to handle this situation. Gosh, I could go on and on.

When I saw Susan in my office, she looked like she hadn't slept in days. Her makeup was smudged, and her hands shook as she clutched a stack of court papers like they were her last hope. She asked me one question.

"Is it time to give up?" she whispered.

That question hit harder than any gavel I've ever heard slammed.

I thought about Kyle—thin, pale, barely 25. Eyes dull. I'd seen hundreds like him. Addicts who'd burned every bridge and pawned every promise. By the time they get to us, they've stolen from everyone who ever loved them. They've lied, manipulated, begged, disappeared, overdosed, and survived.

Later I went to visit Kyle in jail, and when I looked at him, I didn't see a criminal. I saw a broken son and a mother who was breaking right alongside him.

That day, I made a decision as I left—a decision I never expected to make when I became an attorney. I prayed for both of them. Right there outside the justice center, while everyone else was shuffling to their vehicles, I silently asked, "God, what does mercy look like here?"

I knew what punishment would do. Punishment would send Kyle back to jail, this time for probably 20 years. He'd get out eventually, detoxed but not healed, and start using again before the week was out. We'd see him again.

What if grace wasn't weakness, but strategy? What if by extending mercy, we had a chance to break the pattern?

What if, instead of adding another conviction, we added accountability with compassion?

What if we gave him a shot at treatment, long-term, not just time behind bars?

Is mercy risky? You bet it is. You give someone a chance, and sometimes they blow it. But sometimes they don't.

Susan's son didn't change overnight, but that day was a turning point. Instead of prison, I got Kyle into a yearlong treatment center. He stumbled a few times, but he didn't quit. Kyle graduated from a long-term faith-based treatment program a year later…but he never left. You see, recovery did more than just set him free from drugs. It set him *completely* free to choose a different life.

The Bible says, "If the Son sets you free, you will be free indeed" (John 8:36, NIV). Today, Kyle is free indeed. Like many who work hard for their freedom, he chose not to fly off. He stayed in the program, first as an intern and then as full-time staff.

Kyle has used his experience and renewed faith in God to enlist in the war to save others from addiction. As I write this, Kyle is the recovery pastor for a long-term faith-based men's program. He is helping others break free from their chains. He is setting people free.

I've stood in a lot of courtrooms, but for the last ten years, I've stood on the defendant's side of the aisle. Once I recognized that you can't punish the pain out of someone, I wanted to know what happens when justice no longer meets the broken alone, but instead when mercy is paired with it.

I discovered that mercy is not about letting people off easily. It's about giving them a reason to live differently—to heal differently. Once you've seen what mercy can do, you can't go back to pretending punishment is enough on its own.

I began to look at the people our system called "offenders" as sons, daughters, and neighbors caught in a storm of pain they didn't know how to escape. I started to believe mercy and accountability could walk hand in hand and that we can hold people responsible without stripping away their humanity.

But as my eyes opened, I realized something else. Most people didn't see what I saw. They still believed addiction was a moral failure. They thought justice meant punishment, and grace and mercy meant weakness. They didn't see the pain behind the choices. They only saw the choices.

That's when I began to understand that the problem wasn't just what was happening inside the courtroom. The problem was how we were all looking at justice. You see, there's a wide gap between what we *think* justice is and what it actually *does* for the broken. I call this the perception gap, and in the next chapter, we'll talk about that gap and where it comes from, why it's dangerous, and how closing it might be the key to real healing.

CHAPTER 2

The Perception Gap

When I first stepped into the district attorney's office, I thought I knew what justice looked like. It looked like conviction rates, sentences, and the quiet satisfaction of knowing you'd done your part to keep the community safe.

I was brand new and still green enough to think I could fix the world with a well-argued case and a few years of hard work. I showed up in the courtroom with my suit pressed, my briefcase clean, and my view of the world divided neatly into two columns of right and wrong.

Then I met Pastor Tim McLauchlin.

Tim ran a local recovery program, one of the only long-term rehabilitation centers in our area at the time. Everyone in the courthouse knew him. Judges greeted him by name from the bench, and officers nodded when he walked through the hall. You couldn't miss him because he carried himself with the calm authority of someone who had seen too much to be impressed by power.

One afternoon, he asked if he could talk during lunch.

"Can we talk, General Knight?" he said. That's what Assistant DAs in Tennessee are still called.

"Of course," I said.

So that's what we did. He didn't waste time getting to the point.

"I've been doing this a bit longer than you," he said, looking me straight in the eye. "Would you mind if I gave you some advice?"

"Sure," I said. "Let's hear it." I was a brand-new prosecutor, and I figured I could learn a thing or two.

"Your understanding of recovery isn't correct yet."

"What do you mean?" I asked. He'd gotten my attention, and I wondered where this conversation was going.

"I see what you feel when you give people a break, put them on probation, and three months later, they're still using drugs. When they violate their probation by failing their drug screen, you throw the book at them."

"Well, yeah," I said. That sounded about right to me. "I feel like I've given them a shot, and at that point, they've shown me who they are. I heard a long time ago that if a man shows you who he is, believe him."

"That's not how recovery works," he said, his earnest tone compelling me to really think about what he was saying. "Recovery *includes* failure. You don't throw people away when they fall. You catch them and help them get back up again."

I sat there, stunned to silence. No one had ever said anything like that to me before. In my world, failure meant consequences.

If you do the crime, you gotta pay the time. Yet there was a ring of truth to what he said. It unsettled me because deep down, I knew he was right.

I'd seen too many faces come back through my courtroom doors again and again. Every time, it was the same story and the same pain. In the courtroom, we punished the behavior but never did anything to heal the pain that caused it. That was when I started to wonder if I was really part of the solution or just another cog in a machine that kept recycling the same misery.

The conversation didn't change everything overnight. But Pastor Tim's words had planted the seed: justice without compassion isn't justice at all. Looking back, that's where the gap in my definition of justice started to appear—between what I *thought* I was doing and what was actually happening.

I realized there was a big gap between my perception and the reality of addiction.

The Calling to Be Part of the Solution

After that conversation, I started noticing things I hadn't before. Every time someone violated probation and I stood in court preparing to argue for another revocation of their probation, I heard Pastor Tim's steady, patient voice in the back of my mind saying, "Recovery includes failure."

It was easier when I didn't know better. It was easier when I was convinced the system worked perfectly and divided neatly into each column. My black-and-white view was much less messy.

But once I started seeing the people behind the paperwork, I couldn't unsee them.

Some of them reminded me of people I'd gone to school with.

Others reminded me of people I saw every week at church.

A few reminded me of myself.

The truth is, I had become disillusioned long before I admitted it out loud. I still believed in justice and accountability, but the longer I stood in the courtroom, the more I realized punishment alone wasn't actually changing anything.

Men and women cycled through the same courtroom like it had a swinging door. Day after day, I saw names I recognized from old case files with faces that had aged in real time between arrests. It became clear to me that I wasn't stopping the bleeding or healing any wounds. I was just changing the bandage and sending them back into the war zone.

Around that same time, something else began to stir in me. My faith, which had gone quiet for years, started to reignite. The more I wrestled with what I was seeing in court, the louder I heard God's voice saying, "You were made to help, not just to punish." Two questions began to haunt me, day and night.

If I'm going to be there in people's worst hour, what role do I want to play? Do I want to be the one who nails them for what's wrong, or do I want to be the one who helps them put their addiction in the rearview mirror?

It's hard to admit when your job no longer fits the shape of your convictions. But that was the beginning of my shift from a prosecutor who enforced the law to an advocate who wanted to understand the people caught under it.

I didn't know it yet, but I was starting to cross the line between how the world sees justice and how God defines it.

The Jaded System

A few years after that conversation with Pastor Tim, I was standing in a cramped conference room talking with a district attorney friend of mine about whether what we were doing as attorneys was really helping the world. I could tell what I was saying wasn't settling with him. He leaned back against the wall and rubbed his face.

"I guess I'm just jaded," he said, shrugging casually. He said it as if he were just talking about the weather. As if becoming jaded was inevitable. I knew exactly what he meant. We'd both seen the same parade of pain, the same revolving door of defendants.

But something in the way he said it in that moment hit me harder than I expected. It was as if he wasn't just describing himself. He was describing all of us.

If you've ever watched the old Charlie Brown cartoons, you probably remember how the teacher sounded. You knew she was talking, but you couldn't make out the words. It was just background noise, nothing more. That's what the justice system can start to sound like after a while. You stop hearing the people. You stop caring about their stories. You stop believing change is possible.

That conversation with my friend opened my eyes to something bigger than blaming burnout. It wasn't just prosecutors, defense attorneys, police officers, and probation officers who were jaded because they were worn out from their jobs. It was society as a whole because we're taught to act like crime and addiction are normal, expected even. We're constantly fed headlines about failure. Headlines continually broadcast another arrest, another overdose, and another life gone wrong. You can't turn on the news without hearing this same story, and after a while, it shapes the way we see the world.

We stop asking why someone behaves like they do. We stop wondering about what led to the mugshot and start believing the worst version of every story because it's the only version we've been shown.

I refer to the space between what we think we know about addiction and recovery and what's actually true as the perception gap. It's the place where empathy dies and cynicism takes over.

My prosecutor friend wasn't necessarily *wrong* in his view of recovery. He was just basing his opinion on the limited information he had been shown. To him, it looked like very few people whose cases he presided over ever changed. I know many judges, prosecutors, defense attorneys, probation officers, and social workers who feel the same way. If you were in their shoes, you might feel that way too.

Let's pretend you're a judge. Day after day, you sit on the bench and see a never-ending parade of people in trouble. You try to help those you can, so you give some people the opportunity to go to treatment. A few months later, you see one or two of them back in your court. This happens again and again. Is it any wonder if you begin to feel jaded?

Hold on though, you don't have the whole story. There may be four other people you never hear about again who completed their programs. Today, they're working a job and building a career. They've reunified with their families and children and will never step foot in your court again. There are real stories like that happening, but when all you're exposed to are the ones who repeatedly fall short, you naturally believe the process isn't working.

Think about it. When was the last time the evening news began with a report like this: "A Tennessee man successfully completed drug rehab today. Over the past year, he has learned a trade, earned his GED, landed his driver's license, paid off his fines, and regained custody of his two small children."

Never, right? But almost daily, you hear something like this: "A Tennessee man was arrested today for the manufacture, sale, and delivery of fentanyl. This is the man's third drug charge, and he was on probation at the time of the arrest."

These are reasons why I believe it is so important for advocates of treatment to talk about the success stories that we are seeing. I am constantly telling judges and prosecutors about the people they permitted to go to treatment and how they are doing. I talk about their struggles and about their victories. When those same people graduate, I am quick to get them back in front of that judge to present their certificate of completion in person.

To quote a phrase often used, "We have to recover out loud."

And yet…

If I could paint you a picture of the justice system, it wouldn't look like a shiny marble building or a balanced scale. It would look like a 45-year-old man sitting at his desk with his head in his hands, exhausted. He's still showing up and doing his job, but he's carrying more than he was ever meant to hold. Our justice system today is overwhelmed, often ill-equipped, and, at times, heartbreakingly human.

The Truth About Addiction vs. What Society Sees

A few years ago, I wrote and filmed a short documentary titled *Hope Lives Here* about a man who fought his way through addiction and went on to open a men's recovery center just down the road from my home.

When I sat down to edit the video, I decided to open it with a montage of local news clips about drug busts and overdoses with sirens and flashing lights. I wanted story after story after story to flash across the screen in the first 60 seconds.

It's jarring for sure, but I didn't do it for the shock value. I did it to make a point. It's no wonder there's a perception gap when it comes to addiction. We see the worst because that's what we've been conditioned to notice—the same story of another failure, another arrest, and another statistic.

What headlines don't show is that behind every one of those stories is a *person*. Each person is someone's son, daughter, parent, or sibling who's trying to survive a battle most of us can't even imagine.

In the documentary, the leader of the recovery center found freedom from addiction, but he didn't just stop doing bad things. He started doing acts of service within his community. He became the kind of man who spends his life helping others find the freedom he found.

That's the part of the story society never sees. We hear about the failures, but we don't hear about the redemptions. We magnify the problem but ignore the progress. We receive our information in broad, general strokes through headlines and statistics, but addiction happens in one person, one story, and one heartbreak at a time.

When you only see addiction from a distance, it's easy to believe the lie that addiction is a choice. It's easy to tell yourself it's a matter of willpower, and if people wanted to stop, they would. But I've sat across from too many people to believe that anymore. Addiction isn't about choice. It's about *pain*. I believe addiction most often happens as a result of trauma that was never treated and wounds that were never healed.

The good news is that many times when you help someone overcome that pain, they don't just stop doing bad things. They start doing good things. They rebuild. They mentor. They serve. They forgive.

That's what I wish more people could see. When we allow ourselves to see the *whole* story, not just the headlines, the perception gap starts to close.

The Justice System's Limits

I love the justice system. I still get chills when the bailiff calls out, "All rise," and everyone in the courtroom stands. That moment of respect to stand up for the idea that the truth still matters and the law still holds weight is awe-inspiring. I believe America has the best justice system in the world. And I believe that when we stand as the judge enters the court, we as a people are saying that together we can rise above our biases, our anger, and our fear long enough to do what's right.

As much as I believe in that ideal, however, I've also learned that the justice system was never designed to heal people. It was built to enforce order, not restore broken hearts. When we expect it to fix what trauma has shattered, we're asking the wrong tool to do the job.

Imagine trying to hammer nails with a wrench. You might be able to pound a few in, but it's not going to work the way you want it to. Now imagine using the hammer to tighten a pipe fitting. You won't have much success. Both are tools, but when you use them outside their intended purpose, you don't get the result you want.

That's similar to what's going on right now with the justice system. We've handed trauma to the court system and expected it to be the therapist, the pastor, and the parent. It's none of those things, and the system is exhausted. And yet, we keep feeding people through, one after another, expecting a miracle.

People look at what a defendant has been charged with and think their crime tells the whole story. It doesn't. A person's charge also doesn't differentiate between those who actually did the crime they were accused of and those who were falsely or wrongly accused. (Falsely accused means you didn't do it. Wrongly accused means you did something, but not what you're being accused of.)

Being wrongly accused is something that happens a lot when it comes to drug cases. Someone gets caught with a gram of meth, more than the half-gram threshold in Tennessee, and suddenly they're charged with manufacturing, selling, and delivering drugs, which is a Class B felony. But the truth is, a gram of drugs is a day or two's worth at most for that person. The person carrying had no intention of selling the drugs they worked so hard to get. They need it to make it through the next 24 hours.

And if they were selling, it has been my experience that 90% of people selling drugs are only selling to support their own personal habits. They're not kingpins. They're not driving Cadillacs or hauling truckloads of meth across state lines. They're just trying to feed an addiction that is demanding their full attention and consuming them from the inside out. An addict will often buy three grams so that they can sell half to pay for their fix and keep the other half to get them through a few days of their addiction. I'm not trying to justify it, mind you, I'm just trying to explain it. They're just trying to feed their own habit, but on paper, it looks like a drug ring. Then, we throw them in prison and congratulate ourselves for making the community "safer." Yet, we never stop to consider how the punishment impacts the pain that caused the behavior in the first place.

But what if we did? What if, instead of judgment, we chose compassion as the foundation of our strategy?

Compassion Is a Strategy

Justice has a missing piece, and that piece is compassion. The problem with punishment alone is that it can control behavior for a while, but it can't heal pain. You can lock up a person's body, but their trauma follows them inside and still runs free in their mind. For a person stuck in their pain, internally it already feels like there's no way out.

But instead of treating someone's pain, we punish it.

Instead of acknowledging someone's fear, we ignore it.

Instead of helping mend someone's brokenness, we blame people for it.

That's because we've been conditioned to see compassion as weakness, as if it's the opposite of justice. I hate to say it, but this faulty view of compassion is also common among those who profess to be Christians. Despite what the Bible says, despite the clear teachings of Jesus, Americans have a really hard time making compassion a priority. But real compassion doesn't excuse what someone has done. It faces the circumstances, then looks deeper and asks why. Compassion as a strategy is a practical choice that allows you to get close enough to understand what's really happening. When you really listen and take the time to learn someone's story, everything starts to change. You stop seeing a "case" and start seeing a person. You stop seeing an addict and start seeing a life that still matters.

If you really want to understand addiction, you can't do it from a distance. You have to get involved. Go volunteer at a recovery center. Sit with people in safe spaces where you can ask questions and listen longer than feels comfortable. Instead of treating the problem of addiction like it's just another headline, start treating it like a mission. If you don't, nothing will change, and things like the story I'm about to tell you will continue to happen.

Charlie's Story

Charlie* was a veteran who had done everything his country asked of him, only to come home with scars no one could see. I had met his father a few years before, who is a man I greatly respect. Before I ever met Charlie, his father told me, "My son went off to war and never came home."

At the time, I didn't fully understand what he meant. Later, I learned that Charlie had served in heavy combat overseas. When he returned, he wasn't the same. He experienced flashbacks and sleepless nights. Like so many others, he tried to outrun his trauma by self-medicating with illegal substances.

By the time I left the DA's office and started my private practice, Charlie had become well-known to everyone in the system. If an officer needed a quick arrest, they knew he was an easy target. He was often homeless and could usually be found nearby in possession of something he shouldn't have.

When I finally met Charlie, I was struck by how polite he was. He always said, "yes, sir." Even sitting across the table from me in an orange jumpsuit, he still had that soldier's bearing.

"Jail's easier than the outside," he told me, and I believed him. The jail had walls and order and rules. The outside world didn't.

One afternoon, my law partner and I were negotiating cases in a crowded conference room at the courthouse. The room was packed with too many people, too many egos, and too much noise. A dozen prosecutors, defense attorneys, and police officers were all crammed together, arguing over files when Charlie's name came up.

Some of the officers began talking about him and laughing like he was a lost cause. One of them said, "I'm so tired of hearing guys use PTSD (post-traumatic stress disorder) as an excuse for being addicts."

I wanted to jump over the table and knock some sense into him. I knew Charlie's story. I knew his father. I knew the battles Charlie had fought both overseas and in his own mind. What made it worse was how a young officer was standing beside Charlie's critics, nodding along. I knew the young officer was in counseling for his own PTSD. But he didn't say a word, and I couldn't believe it. There he stood, backing the mockery of another man who was fighting the same demons.

That's the perception gap in living color. Even when people share the same wounds, they'll still distance themselves from anyone who deals with pain in a way that makes them uncomfortable.

To acknowledge their pain is to admit, "That could be me." Most people aren't ready to admit that, but for the grace of God, that could be them. Admitting as much would mean they might feel obligated to help, and they're not ready. That day in the crowded conference room, I saw how deep the stigma runs. We don't just condemn people for their addiction. We leave them where they are. The sad thing is, the distance between judgment and empathy is often just one honest conversation we were too afraid to have.

Consequences…or Conversations?

Charlie died not long after that day. I was too late for the conversation that could have made a difference. All I could do was go to another funeral and stand beside his father as he mourned. Then I went back to my office, laminated another obituary, and placed it in the drawer in my conference room. It was time for me to stop pretending this was someone else's problem. The truth was sitting right in front of me every day in the courtroom and in every story of a life that ended too soon.

We can't fix what we refuse to feel, and we can't heal what we refuse to touch. If we want different results, we have to get closer, not colder—and that takes courage. It's easier to scroll past a headline than it is to look an addict in the eyes. It's easier to verbally debate the system than it is to volunteer on a Saturday at a recovery center. It's easier to tell yourself "they should've known better" than it is to sit down with someone who's struggling and ask about *their* life.

Yes, it's easier…but not better. If we really want things to change, we must start by engaging with the people who are struggling with addiction. I believe that it is the only path forward towards healing for all.

That might mean showing up at a local recovery program and serving a meal, or sitting down with someone who's struggled with addiction and just listening. It might mean reading a book about recovery, learning someone else's story, watching a documentary on a life changed, or simply refusing to look away. Passive information gathering will only take you so far. Transformation happens when you get close enough to get involved.

So I'm asking you to take the first step right now.

You picked up this book for a reason. Don't skim it or half listen. Set aside any cynicism or doubt you feel. Hang your protective armor on the shelf. Then read every page of this book and let yourself feel what you've unconsciously spent years learning to ignore.

I dare you to make it to the end of this book and *not* want to do something about what you've seen. Because once you've really looked at the truth and seen the people behind the pain, you can't go back to pretending you don't know.

CHAPTER 3

How We Keep Failing Families

I've learned two things over the years as someone who works in both the justice system and the ministry. First, families have all the heart, but not enough good information. They're full of love and compassion, but they're flying blind when it comes to helping their loved one(s). Second, the people inside the justice system have the information, but so many have lost heart. They *know* all the right things, but they're too jaded or overwhelmed to feel or act.

It's like there's a wide gap between the two, with families on one side and the justice system on the other. Most parents and family members I meet are just trying to do *something*. Anything. They can't stand the idea of doing nothing while their child is in trouble, so they jump straight into the gap. They call anyone they can think of who might be able to help. They beg, plead, cover up, bail out, and fix whatever they can. Their heart is in the right place, but without good information, they often make things worse.

Meanwhile, judges, probation officers, law enforcement officers, defense attorneys, and prosecutors stand on the other side of the gap. They're good, experienced people who know what to do and have the connections to make things happen. But they've often become numb to the cases they encounter. So often, each case is just a number, not a name. Instead of seeing the person, they see the charges brought against them. Our system knows how to sentence a body, but it doesn't know how to mend a soul.

And the families of the defendants? We fail them by letting them fall through the cracks.

For a long time, I was the same way. I saw the defendant in front of me, but never considered the mother crying at home. I saw the drugs, not the damaged soul seeking relief. I handled cases without giving much thought to the chaos that caused them. We referred to drug cases as "victimless crimes."

Then God opened my eyes and showed me the rest of the picture. Families are the invisible victims of addiction. They might not be behind bars, but they're serving a sentence all the same. Behind every addict is a mom who can't sleep, a dad who blames himself, or a grandparent raising kids they never expected to raise.

In this chapter, you're going to meet some of the invisible victims of addiction. You'll read the stories of two mothers whose sons struggled with addiction and learn about Linda, who turned her experience with addiction into a recovery mission. I'll show you what the system and families are getting wrong and how to bridge the gap between the two. Then I'll reveal the 7 Steps to Freedom that help my clients heal their pain and break free from addiction. But first, let's take a closer look at a few invisible victims of the addiction epidemic.

The Invisible Victims of the Addiction Epidemic

When most people talk about addiction, they think about the addicts. They're the ones who get arrested, land in court or overdose, and end up in the hospital. But what I've come to see is that the damage doesn't stop with the addict. There's another group of invisible victims who are deeply affected, and you likely know them well.

They're not on the courtroom docket or in the news, but they carry a sentence of shame, guilt, anxiety, and sleepless nights all the same. Sometimes they even lose jobs, relationships, health, and peace trying to hold everything together while the person they love self-destructs. Invisible victims are the moms and dads, spouses, kids, siblings, and grandparents of addicts that our system doesn't know what to do with.

No one blames them, but they still pay a high price.

When I tell people who don't understand addiction what I do, they don't get it. I can argue science and brain chemistry all day long, but most of the time, it doesn't change a thing. In their eyes, the addict made their bed. Why would addicts need help? But something shifts when I ask, "Do you know their mom? Do you know what she's been through?" Or, "who's going to raise those kids if we just leave them in the ditch?"

We can't just keep passing the pain down the line. If we don't help those who are struggling today, their children could be walking the same path ten years from now. I often explain this to addicts who are parents like this: They can face their addiction and get help today, or they can make their child face it later. Sooner or later, someone will have to deal with addiction. Who would they rather it be—themselves or their child?

I'm convinced that families are the key to recovery. They're the ones who can really help their loved ones either break the cycle or pass it on, but they can't do it alone. They need information and direction. They need people willing to meet them where they are in the middle of their pain, not just in courtrooms or treatment centers.

The good news is, I've seen it work. When families get the right information and the people in the system use their hearts, healing starts to happen. It's not easy, and it's not fast, but it *is* possible.

In the stories below, you'll see the difference a family can make. I've walked through the impact of addiction with both of these mothers. They love their children fiercely and were desperate to help them, but their paths and their outcomes couldn't have been more different. We'll call them Amy and Emily, and these are their stories.

Two Families, Two Paths

I've seen a lot of families walk through addiction. Some come out stronger, and some don't come out at all. The difference usually isn't how much they love their child. The difference is usually what they *do* with that love.

Let me be clear—both moms in the stories I'm about to share are good moms. They love their sons very much. But their stories have very different outcomes.

Amy's Story: The Fixer

When Amy* first found out her son was using substances, it hit her like a punch to the gut. Her first thought was, *How could this happen?* Her second thought was, *How do I fix it?*

Like most parents, Amy tried everything. She searched his room, tracked his phone, followed him at night, and even forced him into rehab multiple times. When he relapsed, she doubled down, thinking maybe this time she could love him hard enough to make him quit.

But that's not how addiction works.

What started as love turned into control. What started as hope turned into exhaustion. She couldn't sleep. She stopped talking to friends. Her anxiety got so bad that she ended up on medication. Every moment of her life revolved around her son's choices, and none of it made a difference in his addiction.

Common opinion told her to use tough love. She should kick him out and let him hit rock bottom. But the spectators weren't the ones sitting awake at 2 a.m., wondering if her son was alive. They weren't his mother. Amy loved deeply, but she lacked good information about what kinds of treatments were available. She was trying to fight a battle she didn't understand.

Emily's Story: The Surrendered Heart

I first met Emily* years ago when she was waiting tables. She didn't know much about me then. I was just some guy who came in with his wife who was kind to her. In the world of waitressing, kindness isn't something people always get, so it stuck out to her. Whenever my wife and I would come in, we'd chit chat and share stories about our kids and our jobs.

Years later, when Emily's son spiraled into addiction, she remembered our conversations and how I'd told her about my work with recovery. She didn't know where else to turn, so she called me. By the time we talked, she was angry at her son, at herself, and at God. She felt like she'd done everything right. How could this still be happening? She wanted answers, and she wanted them now.

Emily and I had a lot of conversations back then. I tried to help her see that what her son needed wasn't a rescue. He needed recovery, and recovery takes time and requires surrender on the part of the addict. She didn't like hearing that at first, but we kept talking.

Somewhere along the way, something shifted. Her anger started to break, and her heart started to soften. She let go of trying to control the process and started trusting God to work through it. When her son finally entered a faith-based program, she didn't see the change in him right away, but she stayed steady. She kept believing, and slowly, her son began to change, and so did she.

Later, she told me she realized God had been answering her prayers all along. She'd been begging Him to give her son back, but instead, He was giving her son a new life founded in Jesus Christ. What gets me every time she tells that story is what she says at the end: "God didn't just save my son's life. He saved mine too." Emily had access to more information about addiction and recovery than Susan, and it made all the difference.

Families like Amy's and Emily's are everywhere, and we can't keep leaving them in the dark. They don't need judgment; they need direction. They need people to walk with them and show them what love looks like when it's guided by truth. When heart and knowledge finally come together, that's when healing begins.

Recognizing the Hidden Damage

For a long time, I thought I understood addiction. As an attorney, I was trained to look at the facts and stay objective. I saw the crime reports, the evidence, and the defendant sitting in front of me. I focused on the problem that needed to be solved—getting drugs off the streets and getting the best outcome for each case. I forgot about the people behind the scenes who were breaking under the weight of it all.

I didn't see the wife at home trying to hold everything together.

Or the mother who couldn't sleep, wondering if tonight would be the night she got *that* phone call.

I didn't see the little boy who kept asking why his daddy didn't come home.

Or the young girl who watched her older sister turn from role model into cautionary tale right before her eyes.

I didn't see the suffering of the invisible victim.

Until God opened my eyes, I didn't realize how blind I'd been. I didn't plan to get involved in recovery work. I just kept seeing the same people come through the system, and I got tired of watching lives circle the drain. What I was doing wasn't really helping anyone. I had to be missing something.

One night I prayed, "God, show me how *You* see this," and He did. Right away, miraculously and supernaturally, I began to see the ripple effect of trauma addiction leaves on family members and future generations. You see, God doesn't see sin the same way we often see it. We see the bad decision and the immediate consequences. He sees that *and* the fallout. He sees the children who get hurt, the broken marriages, and the shame that's passed down like an inheritance nobody asked for.

God opened my eyes to it all, and once I saw it, I couldn't unsee it. I learned that real compassion means being willing to see it all, then stick around and do something about it. That's the kind of compassion someone like my friend Linda Vickers lives out every day.

Linda has never used drugs a day in her life, but addiction still found her through her son and her niece. For years, she was the invisible victim who prayed, cried, and tried to help from the sidelines. When she realized she couldn't fix her loved ones herself, she asked God what she *could* do. He called her to serve women who were ready and willing to accept help.

Linda left her large house in an upscale neighborhood and started a women's recovery center, where she and her husband live in a 10-by-20-foot room so that they can be with these women every day.

"If I can't change what happened to my family, maybe I can help someone else change theirs," she told me.

Today, Linda runs Safe Haven, a faith-based recovery program in the heart of Tennessee. It's one of the most powerful programs I've ever been part of. Every time I walk into that place, I see the fruit produced because a woman said yes to what God asked her to do. The world needs more people like Linda who are willing to bridge the gap so that families can start healing. Oh, and by the way, while she was busy doing the work of ministry, her son successfully completed a recovery program and is still sober—actively helping others today. Her niece also got clean and is a powerful advocate for women's recovery.

How to Bridge the Gap Between Families and the System

Both sides mean well, but while they're both getting some things right, they're also getting some things wrong. Let's start with what families are getting wrong.

What Families Get Wrong

Families almost always lead with their hearts. They want to fix things, to save their child, to stop the bleeding right now. I get it. If it were my son or daughter, I'd feel the same way. But addiction doesn't respond to control. It *feeds* on it.

When parents start tracking phones, hiding money, covering bills, and lying to employers on behalf of their children, they're not fixing things. They've become part of the problem. They're not bad parents. They're just desperate.

Parents and guardians are operating out of love, and they think they're helping. But they don't understand that they're delaying the pain that could finally bring change. Meanwhile, they're carrying around a heavy load of shame that keeps them from reaching out for help. For this reason, many families never get the help they need until it's too late.

What the System Gets Wrong

On the other side of the gap are judges, probation officers, attorneys, police officers, and elected officials who also mean well. Most of them started out wanting to make a difference. But along the way, they got worn down, and it stopped being personal.

They know all the rules and procedures, but as I've said many times, they forget the people. Compassion gets buried by policy because it's easier to move a file than to mend a life. That's where the justice system gets it wrong. The system issues punishments, not remedies. It can label and file away charges for life, but it can't restore a soul.

That's what I mean when I say families often have all the heart and no knowledge, and the system often has all the knowledge and no heart. They're two halves of the whole problem that struggle to meet.

Where Healing Begins

The way I see it, it's my job to help bring those two sides together. When someone comes into my office on a drug charge, I give it to them straight. I tell them that I'll represent them on the legal side, but I also want to help them deal with what brought them here. If we don't address the root issue, we're just buying time until the next arrest, and that's not a solution anyone wants.

Then I ask them questions that not many other attorneys will bother to ask.

"Do you have a drug or alcohol problem?"

"Do you want to break the cycle now, before you lose everything?"

If they say yes to either of the above, we get to work.

At first, helping people get into long-term, faith-based recovery programs instead of jail was just something I did for clients as part of my legal practice. Today, I also help people I don't represent legally. Some people hadn't even been arrested yet. If they're at rock bottom looking for a way out, I will walk with them through the recovery journey.

That's how I bridge the gap. I meet families where they are, help the system remember what it is capable of, and remind both sides that every person with addiction is worth saving. I'd much rather be known for helping rebuild families than helping build more prisons. To start bridging the gap, let's start with the help families need first.

A Parallel Path to Helping Families

When I started walking with people through recovery as an attorney, I realized their families needed healing too. The addiction might belong to one person, but the pain belongs to everyone in the house. That's why I say it's a parallel path. The addict needs transformation, the family needs restoration, and both of them need each other. A lot of that pain comes from not knowing what to do.

Like Susan, Amy, and Emily, families will tell me, "I just want to help," but they don't know what helping should look like. They don't know what to say, when to step in, when to step back, or how to make peace with the things they can't control.

I started teaching families a simple process as I began working with their loved ones. This process helps them walk through the chaos of addiction without losing their hope.

The following steps are what I walk families through as they navigate addiction and recovery with their loved ones. You can borrow these and use them too.

Step 1: Build Rapport and Understanding

The first step is relationships. Before you can help anyone, you have to understand them. I encourage families to learn what addiction is, how it works, and what it does to the brain and emotions. I also urge them to replace judgment with curiosity and listen more than they talk. When families understand what's really happening, they stop reacting in fear and start responding with wisdom.

Step 2: Learn How to Navigate the Justice System

The justice system is confusing, even for those who work in it. For families, it can feel like a maze with no map. They need someone on the inside to come alongside and explain the process. It helps them to know what to expect in court, what options exist, and how to use this season to move toward treatment instead of punishment.

I encourage them that the goal isn't just to get their family member out of punishment. They can use this moment to start turning things around. When families know the system, they stop feeling powerless and can act purposefully with a sense of direction.

Step 3: Facilitate Treatment

The family's heart says, "We want them to be okay."

The system says, "They need a plan."

My job is to get the head and the heart to start working together. I help them look for long-term, faith-based, free programs that offer real discipleship and community. I work with families and talk about what's realistic, what's required, and what happens next. When a family helps get their loved one into a solid program, it gives them a sense of purpose again. They're not helpless observers. They're part of the solution.

Step 4: Provide Spiritual Guidance

Addiction is a spiritual war as much as a physical or emotional one. Families need someone to remind them of that and point them back to the only One who can win it. I spend a lot of time praying with parents, walking them through Scripture, and helping them rediscover who they are in Christ apart from the chaos. When a parent remembers who *they* are in Christ, they stop trying to be God and control things in an effort to fix the situation. And that's where peace starts to return.

Step 5: Walk Alongside Them Through Recovery and Reconnection

Recovery doesn't end when the program does. In fact, that's when the real work begins. When the family member leaves recovery, there's work ahead to rebuild trust, reestablish boundaries, and learn how to live together again. And it's not going to go perfectly from day one.

I tell families that they don't graduate from grace. In other words, they're still going to need a lot of it. I urge them to keep showing up, keep praying, and keep loving, even when it's hard. Sometimes that means welcoming someone home. At other times, it means holding space for them until they're ready to come home. But it always means staying connected to the process instead of hiding from it.

Helping families heal is just as important as helping addicts recover. When both are walking in the same direction toward freedom and understanding, the chances of real, lasting change increase.

The Justice System and a Mother's Heart

What about the justice system? Where do we go from here? Well, I'm convinced that the justice system needs more of a mother's heart.

That might sound odd, but I've seen what a mother's heart can do. A mother's heart doesn't ignore consequences, but it refuses to stop believing in redemption. Behind many defendants are families and friends praying for a miracle. Behind many case files are mothers who haven't stopped loving their children. Until the system starts seeing and caring about the people *behind* the paperwork, like a mother would, nothing will change.

I remember one young man I worked with who had no family, no visitors, and no one writing him letters or waiting for him to get out. When he relapsed, the recovery program I got him into could've kicked him out. Instead, they wrapped their arms around him and said, "You still belong here."

That moment of unconditional love changed everything for him. It wasn't the rules that turned him around. It was grace. Unfortunately, grace doesn't happen like that for everyone.

I make sure it happens for the men and women I work with. I visit the recovery centers weekly, and I tell them, "You're going to see me at least once a week for the next year." And they do. Trust takes time, and if there's one thing people with addiction have learned to expect, it's abandonment.

I show up every week because that's what love looks like in motion, even when it's messy. You can legislate policy, fund programs, and write all the reports in the world, but you can't mass-produce showing up. You can't automate compassion. You have to live it.

I tell my colleagues all the time, "You can keep your mediation. I'll take the kitchen table." I'd rather work face-to-face with my clients around their own kitchen tables. That's where the real work happens over conversations, prayer, and people who feel seen again.

Justice seems cold sometimes, but it doesn't have to be cold to be fair. When we start leading with compassion instead of convenience and let our hearts and our knowledge work together, the system stops failing, and families finally begin to heal. We were never meant to run people through a system and hope for the best. We were meant to stand in the gap between perception and reality for them until they can stand again on their own, and that takes heart.

A mother's heart. A mother's heart sees the invisible victims and refuses to look away. A mother's heart believes no one is too far gone. That kind of heart can change not just a family, but an entire community.

The justice system taught me how to manage outcomes, but it was the families—the invisible victims—who taught me how to love people through the mess. They showed me that grace doesn't mean ignoring sin. It means looking at the whole picture, including the person, the pain, the family, and the fallout, and choosing not to give up.

Being willing to see addiction the way God sees it exposes more than the crime and the consequences. It exposes the wound underneath, and that's what I talk about in part 2 of this book. Once we can see the damage clearly, the next question becomes *why*. Why do people keep running back to what's destroying them? Why do good intentions still end in disaster? It all boils down to pain. Pain is the root and a prison of its own.

PART 2

THE ROOT

Pain is the Real Prison

"The Lord is near to those who have a broken heart, and saves such as have a contrite spirit." (Psalms 34:18)

CHAPTER 4

Anatomy of an Addict

Nobody wakes up one morning and decides, "I want to be a drug addict." That may seem glaringly obvious when written in black and white, but it's an important truth to acknowledge. People don't drift into addiction because they're weak, reckless, or indifferent to the people they love. Drug use doesn't begin because of selfishness or rebellion. People turn to drug use out of a desperate need to escape an inner world that feels unbearable. They fall into addiction because they are already carrying a level of pain they don't know how to live with, and the drug numbs that pain.

Pain is almost always at the root of addiction. Sometimes, that pain is born from trauma. Other times, it stems from loneliness, identity loss, or a hundred other quiet pressures that finally become too heavy to bear. But in nearly every case, addiction begins long before the first pill is swallowed or the first hit is taken. It starts with pain.

Avoiding pain is a universal instinct, as automatic as pulling your hand away from a hot stove. We all have our own ways of dealing with pain. Some of us pour ourselves into work, busyness, or achievements. Others turn to therapy, God, or to family and friends. For many people, especially teenagers, drugs and alcohol are far more accessible than therapy, counseling, or support services. It can take weeks or months to see a professional—but only minutes to get high. When someone is hurting deeply and doesn't know how to cope, the thing that offers the fastest relief often wins.

Before addiction ever becomes a physical dependency, it first becomes an emotional one. The first moment of numbness from fear, anxiety, shame, or sadness that has followed a person like a shadow can feel like oxygen after years of suffocating. The brain quickly learns that the drug stops the pain and immediately categorizes it as a means of survival.

To understand just how naturally and powerfully this progression happens, you first have to see how it begins in real lives. Many times, addiction is seeded in the very earliest wounds, sometimes in the very places where children should have been safest.

The Two Roads Into Addiction

After walking with hundreds of men and women through addiction and recovery, I've learned that while every story is unique, the paths that lead people into addiction usually fall into one of two categories. The first path is built on trauma triggered by deep wounds that start early and shape everything that comes afterward. The second path is quieter, often overlooked, and rooted in emotional pain that doesn't always look like pain on the surface. Both roads lead to the same destination because addiction is never about the drug itself. It's about the pain the drug is numbing.

I want to walk you down both roads so you'll understand your loved one or those you advocate for more clearly. One road is full of obvious suffering. The other is lined with the kind of everyday hurt people learn to hide. But both roads are paved by the same force—pain that has nowhere else to go. Let's start with trauma.

Trauma: Gina's Story

Gina's childhood was marked by fear. Years before she ever encountered a drug, Gina was physically abused as a young child. Her stepfather locked her and her sisters in a closet for hours at a time. The frequent and severe beatings he gave left welts that turned blue and brought blood to the surface of their skin.

What made the pain even more devastating was the reaction of the adult she depended on most. When Gina and her sisters went to their mother for protection and love, she told them, "You're okay." They weren't. They were scared children trying to survive in a home that covered their bruises instead of healing them. Even when her grandmother and father repeatedly called the Department of Child Services, the system failed to intervene. The nightmare continued until the day her mother finally left the man who had terrorized their family.

Experiences like these do more than cause pain. They rewire the way a child sees the world. Gina learned early that the world was unsafe, that pain was normal, that adults couldn't be trusted, and that no one would come to rescue her. She grew up without a sense of safety, without emotional protection, and without the stability a developing brain needs. Long before she ever touched drugs, trauma had already carved deep grooves into her emotional life. Later, when she finally found something that quieted the terror inside her for a moment, her brain latched on as if it were a lifeline.

This is the part families and advocates often miss—addiction often takes root years before the first high. The seeds were planted in every blow, every locked door, every unanswered cry for help. When someone who has carried that level of pain for that long finally encounters something that makes the pain pause, even briefly, the relief feels like survival—like temporary freedom.

It's not just a person here or there. Numerous studies, including the people with Adverse Childhood Experiences (ACE) study have proven there's a strong connection between childhood trauma like abuse, neglect, or unstable home life and substance abuse. Children with adverse childhood experiences were found to be:

- Two to four times more likely to develop an addiction[7]
- More likely to turn to substances early[8]

---

[7] J. He et al., "Does Childhood Adversity Lead to Drug Addiction in Adulthood? A Study of Serial Mediators Based on Resilience and Depression," *Frontiers in Psychiatry* 13 (2022): 871459, https://doi.org/10.3389/fpsyt.2022.871459.

[8] Shuai Cheng, Ying Wen, Lili Liu et al., "Traumatic Events during Childhood and Its Risks to Substance Use in Adulthood: An Observational and Genome-Wide by Environment Interaction Study in UK Biobank," *Translational Psychiatry* 11 (2021): 431, https://doi.org/10.1038/s41398-021-01557-7.

- More likely to struggle with anxiety and depression[9]

But this isn't the only contributor. Let's look at the next couple of stories.

Emotional Pain: Nancy's and Taylor's Stories

On the opposite side of the spectrum are people who didn't grow up in chaos at all. They had stable homes, good families, no obvious trauma markers, and plenty of opportunities. From the outside, their life looked normal and sometimes even ideal. But pain doesn't only come from wounds. It also comes from pressure, loneliness, insecurity, identity loss, and the fear of not being enough.

I've seen many people fall into addiction because they spent their lives trying to be the "good kid," the achiever, the helper, the dependable one. They tried so hard to hold everything together that they never learned how to fall apart safely. When life shifted, say a relationship ended, a child grew up, or depression crept in, they didn't know how to cope with the emptiness that followed. For them, addiction didn't begin in trauma. It began in silence.

Take Nancy, for example. Nancy didn't start using because she was trying to escape violence or abuse. She was trying to escape the pain of losing her identity. When her children no longer needed her the way they once had, she didn't know who she was anymore. That kind of loss can feel just as heavy as trauma. And when someone hands you a pill and says, "This will help

---

[9] Meeyoung Min et al., "Impact of Childhood Abuse and Neglect on Substance Abuse and Psychological Distress in Adulthood," *Journal of Traumatic Stress* 20, no. 5 (2007): 833–844, https://doi.org/10.1002/jts.20250.

you relax," your brain doesn't care why it works. It only cares that it works.

Then you have people like Taylor, who grew up in a loving home but struggled with pressure, relationships, and the need to be liked. She cared deeply about how others saw her and tried to keep up an image that looked put together on the outside, even while she was breaking down on the inside. When she found something that made her feel confident, calm, or accepted, it became the thing she returned to again and again. Eventually, it almost killed her.

Addiction doesn't require a tragic childhood. It only requires pain.

Why These Two Roads Matter

Families and advocates often try to answer the wrong question: "Why didn't they just stop?" The better question is, "What pain were they trying to escape when they started?" Trauma-born addictions and quiet-born addictions look different on the surface, but they operate the same way internally. In both cases, the drug becomes the tool the person uses to stop hurting. In both cases, the brain rewires itself around relief, and the addiction grows until it consumes everything else. It looks something like this:

Pain→Escape→Relief→Repetition→Dependence

Understanding the road your loved one came from doesn't excuse their behavior, but it helps you see them clearly. It helps you separate the person from the addiction. It helps you understand why they ran toward the very thing that is now destroying their lives. Most importantly, it helps you hold on to hope. No matter which road they took to get here, there is still a way out.

The Addiction Spiral

The mechanism beneath addiction is universal. Whether the pain comes from trauma, grief, anxiety, shame, chronic stress, abuse, or a profound sense of not being enough, the path is the same. I call it The Addiction Spiral, and it goes something like this:

1. Trauma creates stress.
2. Stress drives toward drug use and reuse.[10]
3. Stress after use increases and causes more use.
4. Stress is one of the top three things to cause relapse.[11]

Drugs, alcohol, and other substances become the quickest way to turn off fear and numb emotions. The person may not even like the drug itself. They just like who they get to be for a moment when the pain is quiet. That emotional relief is powerful enough to override fear, morality, logic, and even love. Once the brain recognizes that a substance offers fast relief, it begins to crave that silence more than anything else. Relief becomes a habit, the habit becomes a dependency, and the dependency becomes part of their identity.

---

[10] Pablo Ruisoto and Iván Contador, "The Role of Stress in Drug Addiction: An Integrative Review," *Physiology & Behavior* 203 (2019): 62–68.

[11] Rajita Sinha, "Stress and Substance Use Disorders: Risk, Relapse, and Treatment Failure," *The Journal of Clinical Investigation* 134, no. 9 (2024), https://doi.org/10.1172/JCI172883.

But at its core, it all begins with pain.

One of the best ways I know to explain this is by comparing pain to hunger. When you're starving, you don't walk into your kitchen and carefully prepare a nutritious meal, right? You grab the first thing you can get your hands on. You're not thinking about health or long-term consequences. In fact, you're not thinking, you're surviving. That's exactly what pain does to a person. The brain becomes so desperate to turn off the pain that it will take whatever drug is available. This is why addicts often switch substances without hesitation. The specific drug isn't what they're loyal to. They're loyal to relief.

Once the cycle sets in, the brain starts to rewire itself.[12] Stress hormones stay elevated. Emotional resilience goes down. The systems responsible for reward, judgment, and impulse control begin to break down. Trauma and chronic stress make the brain even more vulnerable, especially when those experiences happen in childhood. The younger someone is when pain becomes a defining part of their life, the more likely they are to develop an addiction later on.

After a while, the brain gets used to the drug. Taking substances becomes the only way they know to feel "normal" and keep their anxiety, fear, and pain at bay. The person you love isn't choosing the drug over you. They're choosing the only thing that has been consistently numbing their pain. That doesn't excuse their behavior, but it does explain it. Once you understand that explanation, you're in a much better position

---

[12] Nora D. Volkow et al., "Neurobiologic Advances from the Brain Disease Model of Addiction," *The New England Journal of Medicine* 374, no. 4 (2016): 363–371, https://doi.org/10.1056/NEJMra1511480.

to help them find a path out. Pain is what starts the addiction. But understanding that pain is also what opens the door to healing, compassion, and the right kind of help.

So what do you do next? There are six things you must know to really help a loved one with an addiction problem.

Six Truths Families Must Know

By the time families reach me, they're emotionally, physically, and spiritually exhausted. They've spent months or years trying to make sense of their loved one's decisions and rescue them from disasters. And nearly every family I've worked with has the same question. "What do we do now?"

If you have a loved one who's addicted to substances, there are six truths you need to understand about addiction. These truths will shape everything you do from this point on.

Truth #1: You Cannot Trust an Addict's Decision-Making While They're Using or Newly Sober

Decision-making is always the first casualty of addiction. Everything else, including relationships, finances, jobs, and reputation, fall apart only after the part of the brain responsible for judgment has already been hijacked.[13]

The reality of a brain on drugs is that it's now wired around the hunger for relief. You cannot rely on a drug-addicted person's promises, explanations, or interpretations of what they need. It doesn't matter how sincere they sound. If the addiction is still

---

[13] George F. Koob and Nora D. Volkow, "Neurocircuitry of Addiction," *Neuropsychopharmacology* 35, no. 1 (2010): 217–238, https://doi.org/10.1038/npp.2009.110.

in the driver's seat, their decisions will always bend toward the thing that numbs the pain fastest.

Making decisions as a person who struggles with addiction can be compared to trying to think clearly while you're drowning. At that moment, you're not prioritizing good choices. You're surviving. Period. People with addiction live in that mental state every day.

I see this all the time during conversations with clients who are actively using. Their eyes will drift past me, around me, anywhere except the conversation. They're scanning for opportunity. They're wondering when the next chance to make the pain stop will be. On the outside, they look like they're being rude or are ignoring me. They're not. It's just that their brain is laser-focused on survival, and survival—at least the way addiction defines it—means finding the next dose.

Truth #2: Your Loved One Cannot Think or Act Like a Healthy Adult the Day the Drugs Wear Off

Families often misunderstand this. They assume that once the substance is out of the system, the person should immediately start making responsible choices. But addiction doesn't work that way. The physical withdrawal may be finished in 30 to 45 days, but the damage to their decision-making began at the start of their addiction and can go on for years to come. If someone starts using at age 13 and gets sober at age 29, they will still think and react like a 13-year-old in many areas of life, especially relationships, money, conflict, and impulse control. They didn't get the years of practice they needed to grow those skills. You are essentially dealing with someone who needs to relearn how to live and make better decisions for themselves.

Truth #3: Your Loved One Needs Structure Much More Than They Need Freedom

Most people think love means giving the person space to figure things out, but space is dangerous in early recovery. They need routines, boundaries, accountability, and people who will tell them the truth. They need to be working within a month or so of detox. Work creates rhythm and purpose. It forces them to show up, put one foot in front of the other, and rebuild healthy decision-making skills.

This is why good recovery programs focus so heavily on daily habits. A good program will walk patients through everything, including

- how to handle money,
- how to communicate,
- how to have a healthy relationship,
- how to set boundaries,
- how to choose friends, and
- how to manage stress.

None of this is optional. These are the skills that keep people from relapsing. Almost every relapse I've seen—and this is supported by numerous studies—didn't happen because someone couldn't handle physical cravings. It happened because they made a bad decision that led to stress, and the stress pushed them back to the only coping mechanism they knew.

Relationships are the most dangerous part. The drug is not the number one thing that pulls someone back into addition. I've noticed that the number one contributor to relapse is relationships, especially new romantic ones. When someone starts using drugs at a young age, their emotional development freezes at that moment. When they get sober in their 20s or 30s, they still date like teenagers. They chase attention, overlook red flags, and choose partners who feel familiar. Often, they choose partners who are unhealthy, unstable, or actively using. I've seen more people relapse over relationships than for any other reason. This is why all of these skills, specifically boundaries, in early recovery aren't merely helpful—they're essential.

Truth #4: You Cannot Do the Work For Them

You can care. You can support, encourage, and pray for them. But you cannot want their recovery more than they do. I've seen mothers, fathers, spouses, grandparents, and siblings exhaust themselves trying to drag their loved ones toward freedom. It never works. The person must reach a point where they say, "I can't make decisions for myself right now. Someone else needs to help me." And sometimes, the family needs to reach that same point: "I can't make decisions for them anymore. Someone else has to take over." They're not giving up. They're just stepping aside to allow room for professional help.

Truth #5: Addiction Kills Relationships

Relationships of all kinds, including romantic, friendship, and family relationships, fall apart during addiction. Families are almost always blindsided by this part because they're watching someone they love turn into a version of themselves they don't recognize. They see lying, stealing, manipulation, broken promises, and emotional distancing, and they feel betrayed. I understand why. You've spent years knowing the son who hugged you after school or the daughter who laughed at your kitchen table. It's devastating to watch them become someone who lies to your face and steals from your wallet. But read this carefully: The addiction is destroying the relationship, not the person you love.

Healthy relationships require awareness, empathy, honesty, and consistency. Addiction destroys all four. A person who is constantly starving for emotional relief doesn't have the bandwidth to nurture a connection. They don't have the energy to support someone else. They don't have the emotional clarity to communicate truthfully. Even if they love you deeply, the addiction makes them unreliable and unpredictable because their primary relationship isn't with you anymore. It's with the substance that numbs their pain.

The destruction you're seeing is not evidence that they don't love you. It's evidence that they've lost the ability to act in alignment with that love. Until the addiction is interrupted and treated, every relationship in their life will continue to fracture because addiction doesn't leave room for anything else. But take heart. Your loved one is still in there!

Truth #6: The Person You Love Is Still in There

They are not gone. They are in bondage. And people who are in bondage can be set free.

Your loved one is buried under the pain, the shame, the fear, and the hunger, but they are not gone. I've seen people come back to life after everyone around them had given up hope. I've watched them transform, heal, grow, and rebuild everything they had lost. I've seen them become better parents, better spouses, better employees, and better followers of Jesus than they ever thought possible. If there's breath in their lungs, there is hope.

I've seen this transformation so many times that I no longer doubt it for a second. I've seen men who were violent, broken, and hopeless become gentle leaders in their homes. I've seen women who were convinced they were beyond redemption become powerful voices of encouragement to others in recovery. I've seen sons and daughters return to their mothers, fathers and mothers return to their families, marriages restored, and lives rebuilt from the ashes. When you've witnessed that kind of resurrection over and over again, it becomes impossible not to believe in hope.

One of the most important roles I play in the recovery process is reminding families that the seeds of who their loved one truly is remain intact. You may only catch glimpses of that person at first in a softened tone, a moment of clarity, or a genuine apology. But those moments matter. They're signs that the real person is still there and that they haven't lost the desire to come home. Even in the darkest seasons, I've never met a single addict who didn't, at some point, quietly ask, "Do you think I can ever be myself again?" I always answer, "Yes, absolutely, you can. I've seen it happen."

This is also where the recovery community becomes especially valuable. When families see people at different stages—someone with 30 days of sobriety, someone with six months of sobriety, someone who has graduated from a program—they begin to understand that recovery is not a fantasy. It's not rare. It's not reserved for the lucky few. It's real; it's happening every day, and the same healing that reached those people can reach your loved one too. Testimonies are powerful because they confront the lie that your situation is hopeless. They show you that transformation is possible, and they keep the ember of belief alive when everything in your experience tells you to give up.

I won't pretend the process is easy. It isn't. Recovery takes time, commitment, discipline, and faith. There will be setbacks. There will be moments when old habits tug hard—on your loved one, on the family, and on you. There will be days when progress feels slow and discouraging. But none of those moments mean that your loved one is lost. They are learning how to walk again after years of stumbling through pain and confusion. With the right support, the right structure, and the right boundaries, they can and will rise.

Hold on to this: The person you love is still in there. They haven't been replaced by the addiction. They haven't disappeared. They aren't beyond reach. They are bound, but they are not gone— and bondage can be broken. I've watched it happen enough times to know, without a doubt, that the story is not over.

Once you understand these six truths, you can make decisions based on what will actually move your loved one or those you advocate for toward freedom. That shift is where real healing begins for everyone involved. But before we talk about what *to do* for your loved one, we need to talk about what *not* to do. The wrong response can cause harm both to them and to you. Sadly, much of what families are told or believe, especially the idea of tough love that includes completely cutting their loved ones off, often does more damage than good.

Before we move into the process of helping them heal, we need to look at the next critical piece: how to protect yourself, set boundaries, and stay anchored in love without enabling the addiction. That's what the next chapter is all about. You now understand the anatomy of an addict. You're ready for the next step, which is learning how to walk this road in a way that brings life, not harm.

CHAPTER 5
The Lie of Tough Love

When people hear that I work with addicts and their families, they often assume I must be the tough love type. They assume I'm the kind of person who believes you should cut people off, shut them out, and let them hit rock bottom. Nothing could be further from how I believe God calls us to treat people struggling with addiction. It's right there in black and white in the story of the Prodigal Son found in Luke 15:11–32.

Most Christians know the broad strokes of that story, but if you look a little deeper, you'll see that it contains wisdom for those walking with loved ones through addiction. In the story, the younger son demands his inheritance early, runs off, and wastes every bit of it. He burns all his bridges, loses everything, and ends up literally living in a filthy pigpen because his lifestyle destroyed him. If you've ever loved someone with addiction, that picture probably feels familiar. The recklessness, the waste, the self-destruction, the shame, the spiral downward—it's all there.

But the most important part of the story isn't the son's collapse. It's the father's response.

The father didn't chase after his son or fund his rebellion. He didn't show up at the pigpen with more money, groceries, or fresh clothes. He didn't make excuses for his son or enable the lifestyle that broke him. But he also didn't lock the gate, board up the windows, or pretend he no longer had a child. The father didn't say, "I'm done with you," even though he would have had every earthly reason to feel that way. Instead, he waited with hope, with love, and with an open door.

That's the balance we're looking for and the heart we're called to mirror.

I tell families that their addicted loved one is the prodigal son, and they're to extend love like the father, not judgment like the older brother in that passage. The older brother represents society, and society can be hard on those struggling with addiction. Society says, "You made your choices. Why should I have to deal with the consequences?" That attitude may feel justified, but it never brings healing or frees anyone from bondage. It certainly never brings anyone back home.

The father, on the other hand, understood that helping someone doesn't mean funding their destruction, and setting boundaries doesn't mean shutting off your love. He refused to support his son's time in the pigpen, but the moment repentance came, he was there. When the son lifted his head and took a single step home, the father ran to meet him.

That image shapes everything I do in ministry, in the courtroom, and in my own walk with families. It shows us exactly how to love without enabling and how to set boundaries without abandoning. It teaches us that compassion and accountability were never meant to be opposites. And it reminds us that the role of a parent is not to make the pigpen more comfortable, but it's also not to remove the possibility of return.

The father didn't cut off love or compassion. What he cut off was his contribution to the lifestyle that was destroying his son. That is the model Christ gave us to follow, and it's a far cry from the hollow, worldly version of "tough love" that tells you to sever the relationship entirely.

You may be exhausted. You may feel betrayed, confused, and heartbroken. But if you're a follower of Christ, you don't get to stop loving. You're commanded to love God and love your neighbor as He loved you. God didn't stop loving you even when you were at your worst.

That's the foundation of this entire chapter. Before we talk about boundaries or consequences or what to do when your loved one shows up high at your doorstep again, I want you to understand that your calling is to love them like the father loved the prodigal son. Bring boundaries and wisdom, yes, but never a closed heart. Because if there's no love left and no light, warmth, or safe place to return to, where will they go when they finally come to their senses? Where will they go when the pigpen breaks them?

Someone has to be the father in that story, and as hard as it is, that someone is you.

Should You Cut Them Off?

One of the most common pieces of advice families hear when they're dealing with addiction is, "You just need to cut them off. It's the only way they'll learn." I hear it from friends, extended family members, coworkers, and sometimes even from well-meaning church folks who don't understand what addiction really is. But cut them off from what?

People throw the phrase "tough love" around like it's some kind of biblical command, but most of the time, what they're describing doesn't look anything like love at all. It looks like fear, helplessness, and exhaustion. It almost always comes from someone who hasn't actually walked shoulder to shoulder with an addict through the long, painful road to recovery.

Cutting someone off is not a strategy. It's a reaction. It's what people say when they don't know what else to do. While there are certain things you absolutely *should* cut off, like money, rides, bailouts, and access to resources that fuel the addiction, you should never cut off your love. It's the one thing that actually has the power to draw them home!

I've seen families stop the flow of money and stop paying the bills, and sometimes that was exactly what needed to happen. I've seen parents say, "No, you're not staying here tonight," because doing so would have put other children or themselves at risk. Those decisions are hard, but they're part of good boundary setting. What I have *never* seen work is cutting off compassion, presence, or relationship. Every time a family does that, the person falls deeper into shame, despair, and isolation—the very conditions addiction thrives on.

This is the core reason why "tough love," the way most people define it, doesn't work. You cannot punish pain out of someone. You can't shame them into sobriety, and you can't teach someone who's drowning how to swim by withholding the rope. Families often confuse enabling with loving, and they confuse abandonment with boundaries.

There is a vast difference between saying, "I love you, and I won't support this lifestyle," and saying, "I'm done with you." The first one draws a line that protects everyone involved. The second one crushes the spirit of a person who is already beaten down by their own choices, trauma, and guilt.

When people say, "Just cut them off," they usually mean emotional severing. They mean stop answering the phone, stop opening the door, stop caring. They mean to distance yourself until the person suffers enough to change. But that's not tough love; that's no love at all. If you're a follower of Christ, it is not an option you've been given. Jesus corrected people's behavior without ever withholding His love. He drew boundary lines without ever closing the door. He challenged sin but always left room for repentance and return. If *He* didn't cut us off at our worst—and He didn't—we don't get to cut others off at theirs.

I understand how a parent or spouse can reach that breaking point. When you're hurting and exhausted, shutting down feels safer. But shutting down isn't protection. It is withholding the very influence that might help them come home. You are not responsible for fixing their addiction, but you are responsible for guarding your heart against bitterness and refusing to let exhaustion turn you into the older brother in the Prodigal Son story. You can say no to money, no to staying in your home, and no to participating in the chaos. But you cannot say no to love. That's the part God commanded, and that's the part your loved one will need most when they finally come to the end of themselves.

So let's redefine the term "tough love." Instead of looking at tough love as cutting them out of your life, what if you saw it as cutting off only what fuels the addiction, not what fuels restoration? Tough love, rightly defined, means refusing to support the destruction while keeping your heart open for healing. Like the father in the prodigal story, be wise enough not to fund the pigpen, yet loving enough to run down the road when the moment of return finally arrives.

This is the kind of love that heals. This is the kind of love that shortens the time in the pigpen instead of prolonging it. This is the kind of love we're going to build on as we move deeper into the chapter. Learning the difference between boundaries and abandonment is what will keep you from doing unintentional harm when your loved one needs you most.

Why Tough Love Fails When Pain Is the Driver

The reason tough love fails when it comes to addiction is because addiction is not a behavior problem; it's a *pain* problem. Any approach that treats addiction as a behavioral issue, including the popular version of tough love, will almost always fail. You can't starve pain out of a person until it surrenders. Pain doesn't respond to force. It responds to healing, structure, boundaries, and love. When families try to use emotional distance as a motivator or punishment, they often end up pouring gasoline on the very fire they're desperate to put out.

People with addiction are already drowning in the weight of their own pain. They carry shame, fear, trauma, regret, and self-loathing that are far deeper than most families realize. They don't need anyone to remind them of the mistakes they've made. They know those mistakes better than anyone. When families respond to that pain with rejection or emotional withdrawal, it pushes the person further into addiction because it's their primary coping mechanism.

I've watched this cycle play out over and over again. A parent or spouse will say, "I'm done. They need to learn." They think that by becoming cold or distant, they're creating motivation. All they're creating is despair, and despair is the soil where addiction grows strongest. When someone with addiction hears, "You're on your own," especially from a loved one, they don't suddenly find strength. They collapse deeper into the hopelessness that drove them to use in the first place.

Like we talked about in chapter 4, people start using substances because they're trying to numb pain caused by trauma, loneliness, pressure, insecurity, depression, or identity loss. Whatever the cause, the addiction forms because the drug or alcohol numbs the pain. If pain is the root, then responding to it with more pain can only push them further from recovery.

Shame is one of the strongest relapse triggers in existence because addiction feeds on it. When a family uses emotional punishment to "teach them a lesson," all they're doing is reinforcing the shame that keeps the addiction alive, adding weight to a heart that is already barely holding on.

Something entirely different happens when love with compassionate boundaries shows up. The combination of boundaries and compassion creates genuine turning points. It interrupts the cycle without severing the relationship. It tells the addict that while you won't participate in their destruction, you still believe in their restoration. That belief matters more than most families will ever know.

I've seen people make life-changing decisions simply because one parent, spouse, or friend chose to stay present without enabling. They didn't remove consequences, but they *did* refuse to weaponize them. In a world where most addicts feel completely abandoned, that kind of presence becomes a lifeline.

If you've tried the traditional tough love approach and it hasn't worked, it's not because you failed. The strategy itself is flawed. Addiction doesn't break under force. It breaks under truth, structure, boundaries, and relentless love. That's the type of love we're going to keep building on as this chapter continues.

Boundaries vs. Emotional Abandonment

One of the biggest misunderstandings families have when they're walking through addiction with someone they love is the difference between setting boundaries and abandoning the relationship. People think they must choose between two extremes. Either they "love, love, love" with no limits and end up enabling, or they put up such hard boundaries that they withdraw love entirely. Neither of these approaches works. The real answer is found somewhere in the middle; what you need is love *with* boundaries.

Love with boundaries says, "I will always help you get better, but I will not help you stay where you are. I'm here for you, but I won't help you destroy yourself or us." Holding both love and boundaries at the same time is what keeps your heart soft without sacrificing your safety or sanity.

Boundaries exist to protect you and other family members while helping prevent anything that would prolong the addiction. Boundaries are not about punishment as much as about clarity. Sometimes that means you don't give money because you know where it will go. Or maybe you don't let them stay in your home because doing so puts other people at risk. And if you don't show up every time they call because you need room to breathe and recharge spiritually, that's okay. Those are healthy boundaries because they draw a line between your responsibility and theirs.

Abandonment, on the other hand, is when we withdraw love, presence, and relationship. It sounds like, "I'm done with you. Don't ever call me again," or "You made your choices—go live with them." That kind of emotional severing doesn't heal or teach anything. It simply reinforces the shame that drove the addiction in the first place. When someone with addiction feels completely cut off from the people who once loved them, they more easily fall into despair. And despair is fertile ground for relapse, overdose, and self-destruction.

Learning to love without enabling can feel complicated at first, so let me give you a few examples of what abandonment, enabling, and love with boundaries might look like in real life. Let's say your son comes home and says he hasn't eaten in two days and asks for $20.

Abandonment says, "No, I'm done helping you."

Enabling says, "Here's the money, go take care of yourself."

Love with boundaries says, "You're not getting money, but I'll make you a plate of food right now, and I'll take you to the store myself to buy groceries." You're meeting a legitimate need without funding the addiction. You're protecting your heart and theirs at the same time.

Want another scenario? Let's say your daughter calls and says, "My lights are about to get shut off. Can you give me $100?"

Abandonment says, "Don't call me again."

Enablement says, "I'll Venmo you right now."

Love with boundaries says, "I'll call the electric company." You don't want to hand over the money, but you can verify the situation and pay the bill if that's appropriate. Or you might come to a point where you say, "I can't sustain this environment anymore. You're going to have to move."

Okay, one more scenario. It's a cold night, and your brother, who is known to experience hallucinations when high, knocks on your door, all strung out and looking for a place to spend the night.

Abandonment leaves the door locked and the porch light off as you refuse to answer his calls.

Enablement puts him up in the spare room, even though the last time you did, no one slept much because he ranted and raved about the bugs crawling under his skin.

Love with boundaries says, "You can't stay here tonight, but I'm going to call around and help you find a place for the night. Let me get you where you'll be safe." The difference is enormous. You've preserved the safety of your home while still preserving the relationship instead of leaving your brother alone in his darkest moment with no lifeline.

Love with boundaries is what you see in the Prodigal Son story. The father didn't fund the pigpen, but he also didn't close the gate. He maintained boundaries without abandoning his son. He didn't remove love; he just removed support for the destructive lifestyle. Because he kept his heart open, the son had a place to return to when he finally woke up to the truth of where his choices had taken him.

That's what we're aiming for. Boundaries that protect everyone involved, and love that never disappears. It's not easy, and you won't get it right every time. But this balance is what keeps you from becoming either the enabler or the older brother.

When you have boundaries with love, you're able to provide the accountability with compassion your loved one needs.

Accountability Without Compassion Is Cruelty

Most of the families I've worked with are not afraid of accountability. In fact, they're usually desperate for it. They want consequences that matter so their loved ones can feel the weight of their choices. In a way, they want the addiction to hurt badly enough to force a change.

I understand that instinct. When you've watched someone you love lie, steal, manipulate, or self-destruct, you want something—anything—to snap them out of it. But I've seen over and over again that accountability without compassion becomes cruelty, and cruelty never produces transformation. Let me tell you what I mean by that.

Addiction already brings consequences. An addicted person loses relationships, credibility, money, health, and opportunities. Their life is collapsing under the weight of their choices long before you ever step in. Pushing them harder, yelling louder, or punishing them more severely might give you a momentary feeling of control but will never produce repentance. Those reactions will only produce shame.

The problem with shame is that it doesn't heal, teach valuable lessons, or provide the wake-up call someone needs. Instead of helping, shame destroys the very identity the person *needs* in order to change.

So we need to drop the shame while keeping the accountability. There are consequences to people's actions. Your loved one needs accountability, but they need accountability *with* compassion that provides consequences but doesn't punish by taking away love and the relationship. This requires not allowing anger to fuel your interactions.

Although anger is a valid emotion, if it rules every interaction, it hurts the relationship. Anger clouds your judgment and makes you reactive instead of responsive. Accountability starts feeling more like punishment than protection, and once the relationship shifts into punishment mode, both sides lose. The addict loses hope, and the family loses influence.

Instead of anger, practice compassion. I'm not saying you should just sweep issues under the rug. Compassion is not weakness or looking the other way. Compassion sees the person behind the addiction and refuses to weaponize the consequences already unfolding in their life. Compassion sees the pain and is willing to stand in the gap with hope for a different tomorrow.

Some of the most powerful breakthroughs I've witnessed have happened in moments where accountability and compassion collided. A son calls his mother from jail, expecting anger and blame. Instead, she says, "I'm not bailing you out, but I do love you. When you're ready for help, you call me again."

A husband tells his wife, "You can't stay here anymore because the home is not safe, but I'm not abandoning you. I'll help you find treatment."

A father looks his daughter in the eye and says, "I see what the addiction is doing to you. I cannot support it, but I will walk with you when you're ready to fight it."

Can you see the impact compassion can have? Your loved one needs guidance, honesty, and boundaries, but they also need your love. No doubt about it, that kind of love is hard. It requires more patience and strength than most people think they have. But it's *love* that cracks open the door to change. Love keeps a heart soft enough to receive correction and a relationship intact enough to support recovery.

As we move forward through the rest of this chapter, this balance—accountability with compassion—is the foundation for everything else we'll discuss. They need each other. Without compassion, accountability becomes cruelty. And without accountability, compassion becomes enabling.

Compassion Without Accountability Is Enablement

Many families struggle with the fear that if they show compassion, they're somehow enabling the addiction. "If I'm kind, won't they take advantage of me?" or "If I show love, won't they think I'm okay with what they're doing?" I understand that fear. Addiction makes people unpredictable and is emotionally draining.

But compassion and enablement are not even close to the same thing. Compassion is a posture of the heart, while enablement is a pattern of behavior. One heals, and the other harms. Compassion says, "I love you, and I'm here for you. But you need to be accountable for your actions." Meanwhile, enablement says, "I'll remove every consequence so you don't feel discomfort."

Talk about two completely different foundations! Compassion keeps your heart tender while keeping your boundaries firm.

Enablement tries to rescue someone from the very pain that might eventually lead them to change. One of the most helpful things I've learned in this work is that addicts often change when their pain becomes greater than their fear of change.

If you try to protect them from every consequence by paying every bill, fixing every problem, and providing every escape route, you actually shrink the window where real transformation could happen. You're trying to love them, but the addiction interprets it as support and fuel.

Instead, open your arms without opening your wallet. Give them a meal without giving them money. Listen without letting yourself be manipulated. Show love while still refusing to participate in their destruction.

I've walked with families who thought compassion meant saying yes to everything, and I've walked with families who thought compassion meant saying nothing at all. Both were exhausted and overwhelmed. What brought them back to center was realizing they didn't have to choose between love and boundaries. They could hold both. Compassion gives you permission to say, "I'm not angry at you, but I'm also not going to help you keep going down this road." It allows you to show grace without sacrificing truth.

Compassion is one of the most powerful forces in recovery because it preserves dignity. When you show compassion, you remind the person that they are still worth loving and fighting for, even when the addiction tells them otherwise. When they hit that moment where they're ready to change, compassion has paved the way for them to reach out instead of running away.

Three Steps to Accountability

Not sure how to balance between compassion and enablement? Use these three steps to uphold accountability with compassion:

1. Acknowledge that a wrong has been committed. Provide clarity as needed.

2. Address the consequences. Clearly outline what needs to happen next, but be kind.

3. Show compassion by continuing to offer love and support without enabling.

Every Addict Needs a Place to Return To

One of the most important things I teach families is that every addict needs an open gate. They need to know that when the moment comes, there is somewhere they can turn that won't shame them or shut the door in their face. That's what the father in the Prodigal Son story provided, and it's exactly what made his son's return possible.

If the father had locked the gate out of frustration or exhaustion, the son would have gone right back to the pigpen. That's how it works in real life too. When families shut down emotionally and cut off the relationship, it doesn't make the addict stronger. It makes them feel hopeless. Hopelessness is one of the quickest paths back to the very addiction they're trying to escape.

Having an open gate doesn't mean having an open house. There are absolutely times when you have to say, "You can't stay here," because of safety, past behavior, or the need to protect the rest of your family. But saying they can't stay is very different from saying they're on their own. A healthy boundary sounds like, "You can't stay here, but I will help you find somewhere safe to go." That's an open gate that includes clear limits paired with continued compassion.

If you can't be that open gate because of history or safety or the emotional toll, then someone else needs to fill that role. It could be a pastor, a mentor, or a recovery leader. God never intended for families to carry this burden alone. What matters is that *someone* stands ready to welcome them when they take that first step toward change.

Walking the Line

Loving someone with addiction requires more balance than most people expect. It isn't simply about saying yes or no, helping or refusing, giving or withholding. It's about walking a very narrow line where compassion and boundaries meet and every decision carries weight. And guess what? You are going to make mistakes along the way.

You will draw a line too softly some days and too sharply on others. You will react with emotion when you mean to respond with wisdom. You will get tired. You will second-guess yourself. All of that is okay.

Families put a lot of pressure on themselves to get everything right because the stakes feel so high. They think that one misstep might derail recovery or trigger a relapse. The truth is, no single decision, good or bad, determines the whole story. What matters is the overall posture of your heart and the consistency you keep returning to. If you stay anchored in compassion, if you keep boundaries in place, and if you refuse to let fear or guilt take the lead, you will be far more effective than you feel at the moment.

Walking this line is exhausting. You may need breaks. You may need to step back and say, "I love you, but I can't talk about this right now." It's okay to need a night to pray, breathe, cry, or catch your breath spiritually. Taking those breaks is not abandonment. It's wisdom. A burned-out parent or spouse cannot help anyone. You are allowed to protect your peace, and you are allowed to rest.

One of the most important lessons I learned in ministry is that you cannot pour from an empty cup. Families who try to be strong all the time eventually crumble under the weight. Families who give themselves permission to be human and get the rest and support they need are the ones who stay steady over the long haul. Recovery is a long haul, not a sprint. It's not even a marathon. It's more like climbing a mountain one step at a time with long stretches where the progress is slow but meaningful.

As you walk this line, remember that your goal isn't perfection—it's presence. It's not about being the flawless parent, spouse, or sibling. It's about being the steady one who doesn't enable, but also doesn't abandon. The one who can say, "I won't help you stay where you are, but I will walk with you when you're ready to move forward." That posture changes lives far more than perfectly executed boundaries ever will.

So give yourself grace. You are learning as you go. You are navigating something that tears families apart and overwhelms even the strongest hearts. The fact that you are here, reading these words, trying to understand and respond with wisdom puts you miles ahead of most people who face this battle. Keep trusting that God can work through your imperfect steps to bring about something beautiful in the life of the one you love.

What Real Love Looks Like

Throughout this chapter, we've talked about the dangers of "tough love," the power of boundaries, the need for compassion, and the importance of leaving the gate open. You've learned how to avoid the traps that so many families fall into, like overhelping, underloving, punishing from anger, or stepping so far back that your loved one feels abandoned. You've also learned that you don't have to be perfect to walk this road.

Most families think that helping someone struggling with addiction means they either help all the time or not at all. But real love lives in the middle. That middle ground is full of wisdom, compassion, and steady boundaries. That is where healing begins.

Now that you understand the six truths from chapter 4 and the principles of love-without-enabling in chapter 5, you are finally prepared for what comes next. You're ready to learn what to look for when it comes to getting help in the form of treatment for your loved one. So take a breath. Take a moment to let these truths settle into your heart. You don't have to carry this alone, and you don't have to keep guessing what the right thing is. You have a foundation built on truth, compassion, boundaries, and hope. Now let's take a look at what the next steps to freedom should look like for the addict.

CHAPTER 6

Where Hope Begins

In chapters 4 and 5, you learned a lot about pain, addiction, broken decision-making, and the destruction that follows. I know it's heavy. It should be. Addiction is not a light topic. It's a force that wrecks homes, shatters trust, and pulls families into some of the darkest moments of their lives. But I want you to understand something before we take another step.

Whether you're a family member, part of the justice system, or a community advocate, those chapters were not meant to discourage you. They were meant to prepare you.

If you don't understand what addiction really is or why addicts behave the way they do, you can't help them. You can't set the right boundaries or make informed decisions. You can't seek the right kinds of treatment that will truly help them. Most importantly, you can't hold onto hope without constantly feeling crushed by confusion or disappointment. Clarity brings stability, stability brings peace, and peace gives you the strength to walk with someone through a very difficult journey.

Everything we've covered so far—the trauma, the pain, the stress, the broken decision-making, the relational fallout—has been about laying the foundation for what comes next. You now have a clearer picture of what your loved one is up against, and what you're up against too. But understanding the problem is only the beginning.

The real turning point comes when we shift from understanding addiction to understanding freedom.

I've spent years walking people out of addiction. I've helped men who thought they were too far gone, women who believed they were beyond redemption, and parents who assumed they'd lost their children for good. I've seen the worst, and I've seen total transformation. Somewhere along the way, God made it clear to me that my job wasn't to punish people for their pain. My job is to lead them toward the kind of healing only Jesus can bring. The courtroom showed me the consequences of addiction. But the ministry showed me the cure. I call it 7 Steps to Freedom.

7 Steps to Freedom

Somewhere along the way, what I was doing stopped feeling like law practice and started feeling like ministry. People would come to me with a legal problem, but that was only the surface. The real problem was beneath the pain, the trauma, and the shame that inspired the addiction in the first place.

I'd tried to punish away pain, but it didn't work. Instead, I began to guide my clients toward healing first. Over the years, I started to notice the real things that changed real lives, and I guided my clients through them over and over again until I had the 7 Steps to Freedom.

But how does a formula I use as a lawyer and pastor help you? If your loved one is ready to get help, the 7 Steps to Freedom provides you with a guide to what works. When you approach recovery with your loved one from these touchpoints, you're setting them up to win. These steps also give you an idea of the kind of treatment and recovery program you should look for.

I've written the 7 Steps to Freedom below as if I'm explaining it to a client who's an addict. Most of my clients are in the thick of their battle with addiction. As their advocate, understanding this angle is helpful for you as well.

Step 1: Come as You Are

God has invited you to come as you are and find healing in Jesus. Most people think they have to clean themselves up before they can come to God, but that's backwards. If you could fix yourself, you wouldn't need Him. Healing starts when we stop hiding in shame. Shame is what keeps people sick. Families hide because of shame. Testimonies are silenced because of shame. Leave shame at the door and just come.

Step 2: You Don't Have to Stay as You Are

God meets you where you are, but He doesn't leave you there. Recovery isn't just about staying sober. It's about growing into who God made you to be. Lean into the process of learning to live free, one step at a time.

Step 3: You Can't Punish Away Pain

Most addiction starts as a coping mechanism for deeper hurt that comes with trauma, abuse, grief, loss. If you only deal with the behavior, you'll never touch the wound.

Psalm 34:18 says, "The LORD *is* near to those who have a broken heart, And saves such as have a contrite spirit" (NKJV).

That's the kind of healing you need.

Step 4: Recovery Is Discipleship

Recovery isn't a checklist. It's a walk. It's learning to live differently, forgive, take inventory, confess, and trust again. Most 12-step programs work when they're grounded in faith, but it's not about religion. It's about relationships, learning what surrender really means, and building a foundation of truth that lasts longer than any high ever could.

Step 5: Build a Healthy Rhythm of Work, Faith, and Fun

For a lot of people, recovery is brand new. You've spent so long in chaos that you don't know what normal feels like anymore, so we'll teach you that

- work gives purpose and stability,
- faith gives identity and strength, and
- fun reminds you that joy still exists.

You need to know that you can laugh again, live again, and be sober while doing it. I can't count how many times I've heard someone say, "Pastor Brett, that's the first time I've laughed in years."

Step 6: Stay Accountable

Accountability doesn't limit you. It protects you. Boundaries are where growth begins. You have to be accountable to yourself and to others. That means letting people get close enough to notice when something is off. Good recovery programs have sponsors, mentors, and church families who can spot the danger signs before you crash.

Step 7: Serve Others

I've never seen anyone stay free for long who wasn't helping someone else get free too. Service keeps you connected. It also keeps you humble and reminds you of the battle you've already won. I tell everyone finishing recovery not to disappear. You need to share your stories and stay in the fight. Those who help someone else rise stay standing too.

In Matthew 20:28, Jesus said, "The Son of Man did not come to be served, but to serve" (NKJV). There's healing and purpose in that.

The 7 Steps to Freedom are a way of life that joins truth and compassion to heart and knowledge. When my clients walk these steps, they start to experience true freedom. But what about their families? Who helps them?

Intervention...or Conversation?

Once you understand the type of treatment your loved one needs, the question becomes how to help them take that first step. This is where most families panic. They imagine dramatic TV-style interventions where everyone is crying, reading letters, and surprising their loved one in the living room. That makes for good television, but it doesn't make for good recovery. I don't recommend the surprise intervention.

The real turning point often begins with a single conversation.

But before you ever sit down with your loved one, there are a few things you need to know. These might be the most important pages in this chapter because the success of the conversation depends far more on your preparation than on their reaction.

Let me walk you through the things I tell every family before they talk to their loved ones about treatment.

Don't Have the Conversation When You're Emotional

If you've just had a fight, if your heart is pounding, if your voice is shaking…stop. Do not start the conversation right now.

You might feel the urgency to do it now because you're scared and exhausted. But when emotions are high, clarity and reason disappear on both sides. If you want this conversation to matter, you must enter it calm, prayerful, grounded, and in control of yourself. Notice I said in control of *yourself*. You can't control them, but you can control you.

If you can't sit in front of your loved one without crying uncontrollably, yelling, or being baited into an argument, then you're not ready for this conversation yet. You need a moment to breathe and pray. You're about to walk into a conversation where stability is your greatest weapon, so take the time to steady yourself.

Do Your Homework First

The number one mistake families make is not researching all their options before starting the conversation.

Many families sit down with their loved ones and say, "You need help. You need to go somewhere. There are programs out there."

Their loved one immediately fires back a long list of questions. "Where? What does it cost? Do they take insurance? Do I have to detox first? Can I keep my job? Can I vape? What about my kids? How long is it?"

If families don't have any answers to their loved ones' questions, the conversation is already over. It's not that they don't want help or that they think they don't need it. It's the addiction talking. Addiction will grab onto *any* uncertainty as a reason to delay.

Before you speak to your loved one about treatment, make sure you've done your homework first. Start by reading this entire book, then call programs and ask them the following questions before sitting down for a conversation with your loved one:

- Which programs will be a good fit?
- What does each program cost?
- Is detox required off-site before entering?
- How does the intake process work?
- How quickly can your loved one get in?
- What does the first week look like?
- What boundaries and rules are enforced?
- What will happen to their current responsibilities, like their job, pets, or children, while they're in treatment?

Information gives you confidence, and confidence gives the conversation direction. Without it, you're walking in with hope but no plan. Addiction can make people very manipulative. If you're not prepared, your loved one could dismantle your hope in seconds.

Expect and Prepare for Manipulation

People with addiction often become masters of emotional manipulation. They don't set out to be that way, and most aren't doing it maliciously. But when a person is trapped by addiction, they're scared, ashamed, and trying to protect the little control they think they have left. That fear will come out in conversation through phrases like:

> "You don't understand what I'm going through."
>
> "You just want to control me."
>
> "Other people are worse off than me."
>
> "I can stop anytime."
>
> "It's not that bad."
>
> "You're supposed to love me."

If you're dealing with your child, your spouse, your parent, or your sibling, they know your weak spots. They know your history and the things in your relationship that you feel guilty about, and they may use them. You must go into the conversation emotionally steady enough to respond without getting pulled into the old dance.

Be ready with phrases like the following:

"I understand that's how you feel, but I also know people who have recovered."

"I may not have lived what you've lived, but I do know what healing looks like."

"I am not here to fight with you. I'm here to help you take the next step."

The moment they pull you into defending yourself, the conversation collapses. You're no longer talking about their addiction. You're talking about your relationship history and that's not where the focus needs to be right now.

Stay steady, centered, and focused. One thing that can help is having support. It's okay to ask people you trust for help. You don't have to have the conversation with your loved one alone.

Don't Have the Conversation Alone

There are families who ask me to sit with them during these conversations. They love their person, but they know they are too emotionally close to remain neutral, and they're afraid they'll be asked a question they can't answer. Both are legitimate concerns, and I'm more than happy to be there for the families I work with.

In fact, I don't always go alone either. Sometimes I bring someone with me who has been through addiction. By the grace of God, I've never fallen into addiction. There are moments when a person struggling will look at me and say, "You don't know what withdrawal feels like. You've never sat on the cold floor throwing up in a toilet from it."

They're right. I haven't. I've never been through withdrawal, and I don't know what that feels like. But I explain that I've helped hundreds of people get free from addiction, and I *do* know how to help them heal. Then I say, "If I have cancer, I don't ask my cancer surgeon if he's ever smoked. I ask him if he knows how to treat me."

If hearing that from me doesn't help, then I can turn to the person I've brought with me who has lived through addiction and recovery so they can say, "I *have* been where you are. Recovery is real, and you can get through this."

What NOT to Do

You want the best for your loved one. It's hard not to let your desire for them to heal take over the conversation, especially if it doesn't go the way you hoped. But it's important to lead with love. Don't unload every frustration from the last ten years. Don't shame, threaten, or try to manipulate them. Yelling and crying hysterically tend to derail the conversation quickly, so try to remain as calm as possible. Don't give ultimatums you won't follow through on. You cannot punish someone into recovery.

Punishment doesn't heal pain. Only Jesus can do that.

What If They Say "No"?

Most addicts say no the first time family members approach them about treatment. But don't give up. No doesn't necessarily mean never. No often means "I'm scared," "I don't believe I can change," or "I don't know who I'll be without this."

Your job as their loved one and advocate is to stay steady, maintain your boundaries, and prepare for the next conversation. Keep praying and learning, and keep the invitation to conversation open. Hope doesn't always move fast, but it does move.

Remember that it's not up to you to save them. What you *can* do is lead them to the place where healing begins. As their advocate, you play a key role in their recovery. Your steadiness may be the thing God uses to open their heart to the idea of treatment. Your preparation and compassion may soften their fears and put their excuses to rest. Your boundaries may protect them (and you) long enough for them to choose help. When they are ready, you'll already have the answers, the plan, and the path laid out. Hope begins not with pressure, but with preparedness.

Up Next in Part 3

Everything we've walked through so far has been about understanding addiction, guarding your heart, and helping your loved one step toward real recovery. But families aren't the only ones trying to navigate this battle. Right now, inside courtrooms across the country, judges, prosecutors, defense attorneys, and members of law enforcement are trying to answer the same question you are: How do we help people find real freedom instead of recycling them back through the system?

I've had a front-row seat to that struggle. For years I stood in the courtroom with a gavel on one side and grace on the other, trying to figure out where justice ends and mercy begins. Part

3 is where I want to show you what happens in that space. I'll cover what the justice system is already doing, where it falls short, and how families can come alongside it. It's also where I'll tell you how I discovered an unexpected doorway of hope within the legal system itself that changed the way I practice law and the way I fight for people who are ready for a better sentence.

PART 3

THE LIGHT

Mercy in the Courtroom and Beyond

"Therefore, if anyone is in Christ, he is a new creation; old things have passed away; behold, all things have become new."
(2 Cor 5:17)

CHAPTER 7

A Better Sentence

I've seen the same scenario play out time and time again among people who have been struggling with addiction for years. After being in and out of jail and detox multiple times, they've made and broken promises and burned bridges. Now they're looking at a prison sentence for drug-related charges, and they're scared enough to be honest. For the first time in a long time—maybe ever—they say the words families pray for.

"I need help."

When someone who needs help asks for it, it's important that the wheels start turning toward a solution. But within the justice system, all too often that's not what happens. The US court system offers some options, but the need is too great.

I respect our justice system and the judges and prosecutors I've worked alongside. Some of my closest friends are the very people running these court programs, and they've poured themselves out trying to do the right thing inside a limited structure. As helpful as drug and recovery courts can be, they can't handle the sheer volume of people who need recovery.

This chapter is not meant to be a criticism of those programs. It's an honest look at the limits of what the system can do by itself and how something different—something *you* can get involved in—can help provide a solution. Let's start by looking at what's available in the US court system.

Where Court-Run Programs Fall Short

The US justice system has drug courts and recovery courts with helpful programs. In some states, there are also veterans' courts and mental health courts with programs. Judges and prosecutors who care deeply are doing everything they can to get people help within the structure they've been given. Unfortunately, there are several reasons why court-run programs alone aren't the complete answer.

First of all, there aren't enough programs to meet the need. How bad is the substance abuse problem in the US today? According to a 2023 survey by the Substance Abuse and Mental Health Services Administration (SAMHSA), 48.5 million people aged 12 and up had a substance use disorder (SUD) in 2023, yet 85.4% (41.4 million) did not receive substance use treatment.[14]

Second, court-run programs are limited by federal and state regulations that aren't always in the best interest of the addict. By definition, these programs can't incorporate faith, which is something I've seen to be absolutely vital to long-term healing

---

[14] Substance Abuse and Mental Health Services Administration, *Key Substance Use and Mental Health Indicators in the United States: Results from the 2023 National Survey on Drug Use and Health* (Rockville, MD: Center for Behavioral Health Statistics and Quality, Substance Abuse and Mental Health Services Administration, July 2024), https://www.samhsa.gov/data/report/2023-nsduh-annual-national-report.

and success. They're also required to allow patients to take opioids or opioid drug alternatives if they have a prescription, which I believe can be detrimental to their recovery.

Third, court-run programs weren't built to provide long-term help after recovery. Recovery is not a two-week issue. It's not even a 90-day issue. You can detox someone in three months and get the drugs out of their system, but it takes time to rebuild character, healthy habits, and self-respect. Court-run programs aren't equipped to build the kind of community that carries someone when the program ends.

Community is the piece most people miss, and it might be the most important one. If we send people who have struggled with addiction back into society without long-term support, how can we expect them to succeed? A judge, no matter how good-hearted a person, won't be at a defendant's kid's birthday party. The prosecutor won't take calls at 1:00 a.m. from a recovering addict who's shaking and sweating and trying not to relapse. They shouldn't—that's not their role. When we put all the responsibility on the court system to provide solutions, we're expecting too much.

Recovery is not just a courtroom issue. Recovery is a *community* issue. That's why I prefer community-based recovery systems, especially faith-based recovery centers. In these programs, community is built into the process and is an important part of the cure.

The Cost of "No"

For the sake of this chapter, let's say your loved one meets the criteria and qualifies for a court-run program. In the jurisdiction where I work, they still must get the approval of the district attorney's office. If the DA's office says no, and they often do, that no is final.

Imagine what a no like that does to a person who has been in a drug spiral for 10 or 15 years. They've been seen multiple times by the police, the prosecutors, and the court. Everybody's tired of them. Now they're finally saying, "I need help to get healthy. Can you help me?" and get an impersonal, "No."

That kind of rejection doesn't just delay recovery or frustrate families. It reinforces an identity that addiction has already seared into the addicted person. "I'm no good. Everybody's throwing me away. Society doesn't want anything to do with me anymore, and there's no hope for me."

A dangerous shift can occur in a drug addict's mind when options run out. They start thinking, "If society doesn't want me, then I don't want society." They stop caring about consequences because consequences are all they've ever known. When that happens, incarceration becomes the only option because it's the only tool left. If jail or nothing is the only answer they get, then we shouldn't be surprised when an addict stops trying.

What am I suggesting then? No incarceration? What about the consequences? Let's talk about it.

What About the Consequences?

In my mind, the question isn't, "Should there be consequences?" Of course there should be consequences. People do wrong things. Addiction causes real harm. But what happens when you put a little mercy and grace inside those consequences? That's what I'm going to talk about in this chapter.

Should a person serve time if they've committed a serious crime? Often, yes. But when it comes to freeing people from drug addiction, we need to step back and look at sentencing through the lens of *where* the sentence is served. We need to ask what kind of sentence has the best chance of producing a different life on the other side.

I started asking those questions not long after I left the district attorney's office and became a defense attorney. I had already realized that straight-up punishment wasn't working to get drugs and drug-related crime off the streets, and I was very limited in what I could do to help people trapped in drug addiction as a prosecutor.

Remember the story about Charlie in chapter 3? I met him very early in my time in private practice. His case was one of the first cases that made me realize something was missing in the current system. At the time, I didn't know what it was, but I knew there had to be a better solution. I began earnestly looking for answers, and that's when I first encountered a real solution—furloughs.

In the rest of this chapter, we'll walk through what furloughs are, how they work, and why I call furloughs the better sentence.

The Furlough System

A furlough is a legal mechanism that allows a person who has already been sentenced to serve some of that sentence somewhere other than a jail cell. Historically, furloughs have been given under very specific conditions, like a medical procedure or bereavement, and they have very real consequences if violated. I, and others in the justice system, began to realize if we could furlough someone for surgery, why couldn't we furlough someone for recovery?

For addicts with drug-related criminal charges, a furlough satisfies what the court needs in terms of accountability and consequences. Meanwhile, it provides the recovery environment the addicted individual needs with structure, community, and a real path toward restoration.

A furlough is a better sentence for drug addicts because it allows them to serve their time in a place where they can get help, find healing, and experience real change, and it does so while also relieving the state of the financial burden of housing in a traditional jail environment.

The instance of the furlough system as a solution that really clicked for me was when I saw my client Kyle go through it and come out the other side. I told his story from his mom Susan's point of view in chapter 1. Kyle struggled, getting arrested repeatedly, going back and forth to short-term treatment, then relapsing again. He reached the point where he was headed for some serious prison time if he didn't get off the path he was on, and I knew prison wouldn't help him get clean.

I got Kyle into a yearlong treatment center, and it completely changed his life. When I saw his transformation, for me, there was no going back. Furloughs work, and that year I helped place 48 people into long-term faith-based treatment programs.

Walking Through the Furlough Process

I've helped many clients like Kyle achieve recovery and restoration through alternative sentencing and furlough agreements. It usually goes something like this story:

A man, let's call him John, stands before a judge on criminal charges for theft and drug possession. He pleads guilty to the charges, and he knows he's earned some real consequences. The judge sentences him to four years. Up until now, you might have assumed that those four years should be served in a cell. For someone with a drug addiction, that isn't the only way a sentence can be served.

With me as his advocate, John has an advantage, and the judge he's standing before is familiar with the furlough system. When the judge, the DA, and I meet to discuss sentencing, I make a motion that John serve the first year of his sentence in a long-term treatment facility. The DA and the judge have seen the success my clients have experienced in faith-based recovery programs, so they agree.

John is given the news that his first 12 months will be spent in a treatment program. When he successfully completes the yearlong program, the rest of his sentence will be revisited by the judge. The goal of an agreement like this isn't only to punish John for what he's done. It's to also heal him from addiction, which is the driving force for his criminal actions. The conviction still stands, but instead of putting John in a cell, where it can be easy to continue to get drugs, we put him in the right kind of recovery program—one that provides a structured environment.

Finding the Right Program

A furlough is a strict, court-ordered sentence with paperwork, accountability, and tracking. If the individual doesn't follow the rules or leaves the program, they're sent directly back to jail. A furlough isn't an escape from consequences. It's choosing a consequence that will save John's life.

A furlough only works if the program is legitimate, structured, and reports well. The system is built on accountability, and a good program has rules, supervision, and documented progress; documentation when someone breaks rules, and clear communication with the court and probation system.

If the program isn't well-structured, a person can do all the right things and still end up violating their furlough conditions if the program doesn't send in the right reports and updates. That's why I always tell families that their loved one doesn't just need *a* place. They need the *right* place. One that protects them not just from relapse, but from the system accidentally crushing them while they're trying to change.

The Anvil and the Carrot

The furlough system works because it's based around what I call the anvil and the carrot. John experiences the anvil and the carrot firsthand when he reports for his sentencing with the judge.

"Look," the judge says, "You've been convicted of your crimes, and I've already sentenced you to serve four years. However, I have agreed to allow you to serve the first 12 months of your sentence at a long-term, faith-based recovery center. I've already found you guilty and sentenced you. There's no reason you'll ever be in front of me again. If for any reason you do not complete the recovery program—and I don't care whether you get kicked out because you didn't follow the rules or you leave because you just don't like their rules—you will serve the rest of your sentence in jail."

That's the anvil, and it represents the real consequences that will happen if John doesn't follow the furlough guidelines. The consequences are clearly outlined, leaving no question about what will happen if he doesn't stick with the program or gets kicked out. This is a level of clarity most addicts have never had, and it helps them stay the course when their cravings try to take over, and they want to quit, which happens to everyone at least once during their recovery. The carrot comes in a moment.

Most people who've never walked through addiction think relapse happens because people don't want freedom enough. I don't think that's true. Sometimes relapse happens because freedom hurts at first. It hurts to feel again. It's not fun to have to face what you've done and sit in the truth without numbing it. The consequences of giving up can provide the reason for them to hang in there for one more day. Furloughs aren't all anvil though. John also experiences the carrot that day.

"However," the judge continues, "if you do complete this program, once you graduate, contact your attorney. Let your attorney know you've graduated, and he'll get you back on the docket in front of me. Come back here with your certificate in hand. Show me you've graduated, and tell me how your life has changed. If I can see a difference in you, I will transfer the remainder of your sentence to an early release order so you can serve the rest of your sentence on probation. You won't have to go back to jail if you obey your probation terms."

What a carrot, right? That judge has just handed John a heaping helping of hope. What John doesn't realize is I've seen this judge go even further and waive fines when there is real progress being made so that graduates can get a better start. Now John knows that when things get tough in treatment, he has a future if he stays. There's a future ahead of him, and things will get better.

Why Furloughs Are Worth Fighting For

"Does it work?" is one of the most common questions I get asked. When people ask me that, they're usually also asking the following:

- Do furloughs stop people from reoffending?
- Do furloughs save money?
- Do furloughs actually change anything beyond the person in front of the judge?

Research shows that when you take someone with a substance problem and place them in a structured, accountable treatment model instead of the standard cycle, you don't just get better stories. You get better outcomes.[15]

When a long-term furlough program is structured and the court partnership is strong, the success rate can be strong

---

[15] National Institute on Drug Abuse, *Principles of Drug Abuse Treatment for Criminal Justice Populations: A Research-Based Guide*, 3rd ed. (Bethesda, MD: National Institutes of Health, 2018), https://nida.nih.gov.

enough that it changes the math for everybody involved. From a strictly practical viewpoint, it costs less than the cost of doing nothing and pretending jail is treatment.[16]

Most of us aren't that cold though. We know the cost of addiction isn't just a line item in a jail budget. The cost of addiction includes emergency room fees, stolen property, and more. Meanwhile, kids are growing up in chaos-filled households, probation officers drown in heavy caseloads, and law enforcement officers keep running to the same addresses over and over again.

Don't forget about the high cost of funerals.

A human being can be more than their worst day. Consequences can carry mercy inside them. The furlough system provides a way to keep accountability intact while still building a bridge to freedom and restoration. Plus, furloughs don't just save one person. Alternative sentencing programs like furloughs save addicts from

- repeat offenses and re-arrests,
- recurring jail costs,
- time spent in court, and
- future family destruction.

Drug addiction causes a ripple effect of damage in communities, families, and the court system. When someone stays trapped in addiction, it spreads outward—more harm,

---

[16] National Institute of Justice, "Drug Courts," accessed March 5, 2026, https://nij.ojp.gov/topics/courts/drug-courts.

more costs, more instability. But the good news is, the ripple effect works both ways.

When someone gets well, it radiates outward in terms of fewer crimes, fewer victims, and fewer children growing up watching a parent disappear. One person's healing can stabilize a whole family system. That kind of stability doesn't just save money. It changes generations.

Not everyone completes a recovery program, but most do. Around 85% of the hundreds I've worked with that received furloughs complete treatment and about 75% are still clean after five years. They don't go back into the system. They become tax-paying, law-abiding citizens with purpose-filled lives. The 15% who don't complete the program go back to jail, not the streets, where they safely finish out their sentence. They were at least given a real shot at not ending up back in the system.

Furloughs aren't about "being soft." They're an honest solution that's desperately needed. The justice system can't keep handing out the same sentences and expecting a different result, only to act surprised when the same person shows up in the system again.

We must choose a better sentence—one that still holds people accountable, but finally gives them a real chance to come out the other side as a functioning member of the community.

Speaking of coming out the other side, what about those who get out of prison clean, only to be thrown right back into the real world? Once their sentence has been served, the journey to staying clean is just beginning. In the next chapter, I'm going to reveal how treatment programs can help people on the other side of incarceration too.

After Incarceration

You probably picture someone getting released from prison like it happens in the movies. The former inmate walks through the gate into the sunlight clutching a paper bag with their belongings. They take a deep breath, embrace the crowd of loved ones waiting nearby, and head out into a brand new start.

The truth is, that's very rarely how it goes. The reality is, many releases are a whole lot uglier and inconvenient for the one being released.

Many times releases take place just after midnight when a person's sentence ends, and the funding for that individual shuts off. So the system moves the problem from *inside* the building to *outside* the building.

It could be the middle of winter, but they'll be wearing the same shorts and t-shirt they were arrested in. To make matters worse, a lot of these folks don't have family. If they do, they probably burned that bridge long ago, so they have no ride, no money, no phone.

But that's where one of the most hopeful parts of this whole story shows up. While the system is busy closing out a budget line, there are people who treat that midnight release like a mission field. Like my friend Linda Vickers, who runs Safe Haven—a powerful women's recovery center. I spoke about her earlier in the book. She goes into the jail to hold Bible studies and do recovery work with inmates, and she's one of the people who answers those middle-of-the-night calls.

"Miss Linda," the voice on the other end of the line says hesitantly. "I know it's one o'clock in the morning, but they just let me out of jail, and I don't know where I'm supposed to go."

"Okay, I'll be right there," Linda says. "You have somebody who loves you. You're not alone."

For someone battling addiction, release isn't simply the end of punishment. It's a dangerous handoff. If no one is there to help support the former inmate's continued recovery, at the first challenge, they'll likely bounce right back into the same old patterns. After all, where else can they go but back to the same people and places that are familiar?

The truth is, we're missing a crucial step if we overlook those coming out of incarceration. There's an opportunity hiding inside the release period. Treatment can begin in the midnight hour when the jail door shuts behind a newly released inmate and they realize they don't have a plan for what comes next. Those who knew where to turn had someone meet them where they were before they ever walked out from behind bars. They had an advocate who showed up, built trust, and told them they never have to go back to where they've been.

These advocates are so important because most people refuse to see prisoners. They choose to believe that jail will provide all the treatment and help they need. I hear over and over again when I'm promoting furloughs to prosecutors: "They can get treatment while they're in jail." However, more often than not, there's nothing available. Even when there is, it's not the kind of consistent, structured, life-rebuilding work people who struggle with addiction need. There is no lasting community, no aftercare, no accountability outside of jail, and no healing of trauma that triggered this entire process.

And the truth is, just because someone is locked up doesn't mean they're sober. Drugs get into jail. I've had people tell me it was easier to get drugs inside than it was on the street. So what do we do? How do we help those who didn't get a furlough before serving their sentence? Let's start by talking about what's available.

Parole, Probation, and Voluntary Treatment

When treatment *does* start on the back end, I usually see it happen in one of three ways.

First, parole. Most inmates serve a portion of their sentence in jail, then the remainder on parole. A parole board can agree to let someone out on this condition: for the first stretch of time, inmates can complete a recovery program at a state-licensed program.

Second, probation. Treatment after probation is sentenced in a similar form, but under a different authority. That's when treatment becomes a condition of probation, and that means the treatment program has to report. The good programs send updates, drug test results, and track community service hours. This is important because if the reporting falls apart, probation officers start seeing it as a sign of noncompliance, even if the person in treatment is following the program.

Third, voluntary. Voluntarily deciding to go to treatment after release also happens, and more often than you might think. Many inmates realize that if they go back to what they were doing, they'll go right back to jail. They recognize the pattern and proactively choose a program to help them break the cycle.

When God Shows Up in Jail

For people who voluntarily seek treatment after release, their decision to get help after jail takes place while they're still *in* jail. That most often comes about because somewhere along the line, somebody showed up for them.

I've learned over the years that there are two different sides to this work, and they're both necessary. A lot of what I do tends to be frontside. I meet people before sentencing, or early in the sentence, when the court is still deciding what's going to happen and there's still a window to advocate for a better path.

The advocates who go into jails and prisons—people like Linda Vickers, Deanna Jenkins, Renee Hill, and so many other names too numerous to list—are doing the back side work. They're putting in the long, quiet hours that happen during incarceration that carry all the way into reentry. They're the ones building trust inside the walls, planting the idea of change before release ever comes, and then answering the phone when somebody walks out at midnight with no plan and no place to go. In a lot of cases, I can help get the door opened on the front end, but they're the ones who help a person walk through it on the back end when it really counts.

Treatment can start anywhere. Nobody illustrates how important this is more than my friend Rhonda.

Treatment Can Start Anywhere: Rhonda's Story

When I think about a life that shows the whole picture of trauma, addiction, felony consequences, and the kind of redemption that turns into a mission, I think about Rhonda.

Like most people who come to struggle with addiction, Rhonda's story starts with trauma. Rhonda experienced the kind of trauma that makes it hard to trust anybody, hard to feel safe, and hard to believe you're worth saving. The brutal childhood abuse she went through is the kind of pain that doesn't politely stay in a person's past; it followed her into adulthood and shaped her choices.

When Rhonda slid into addiction, it wasn't because she woke up one day and said, "I'd like to ruin my life." Addiction offered numbness, something that felt like relief from the pain. For a while, she survived inside that numbness, but then the drug world and the system caught up with her.

Rhonda didn't get hit with the kind of charges people expect. She was a rarity because she didn't have major drug charges. She was charged with money laundering. The way it happened sounds like a movie. Her boyfriend, a big-time dealer, got arrested. In order to keep his operation going, he instructed her to dig up buried cash. One day, she got pulled over with $100,000 cash in her trunk, and it smelled an awful lot like dirt.

That's not a small mistake. That's a felony.

Knowing she had a drug problem, Rhonda applied to a faith-based rehabilitation program before her sentencing. During the interview, the director asked her a question that got to the bottom of everything: "Why should we accept you?" Rhonda didn't give a polished answer. She broke down and admitted she felt worthless and needed help.

People can argue theology, policy, and program models all day long. But I've sat across from enough addicted men and women to know how much that moment of honesty matters. You cannot build a new life on top of a lie. The kind of honesty that finally admits, "I can't do this, and I can't save myself" is where real change can begin.

Here's the part that makes Rhonda's story a 180-degree proof for me.

I was on the other side of her story in the beginning. Back then, I was working with the District Attorney's office and the drug task force. I was part of one of the task forces that arrested her and her boyfriend.

But years later, God brought us back around into the same orbit. This time, I wasn't standing on the prosecution side of the aisle. I was walking with her through recovery, baptism, and graduation. I stood with her when she went before the judge with her certificate in hand.

Then I got to watch her do something that still stops me in my tracks. She didn't just graduate and move on. She stepped into advocacy. I walked with her through training to become a Certified Peer Recovery Specialist, and she began to use her story as a lifeline for other people.

Now Rhonda goes into prisons doing jail ministry, building trust while being the kind of person inmates will actually talk to.

So why does creating connections that lead to people getting help after incarceration matter?

Because when a woman in a jail pod finally raises her hand and says, "I need help when I get out," she's not looking for a lecture or a brochure. She's looking for someone to believe in her who knows what she's been through. She's looking for someone like Rhonda.

Rhonda's story is a real-life illustration of why advocates and the back-end work they do to help people during incarceration and into reentry are so needed. They can be the difference between somebody repeating the same cycle or finally finding a way out.

The Ripple Effect of a Better Release Plan

I want to end this chapter where we started "Your sentence is up. Good luck. Get out."

When we dump people out with no plan and no support, we create more problems than we solve. We don't just risk people relapsing. A bad release plan doesn't just hurt the person getting released. It spills into homes, neighborhoods, courtrooms, and jails. We risk new victims, new charges, new court dates, new overdoses, and families getting wrecked all over again.

But the ripple effect can run the other direction too.

Because there are roles regular people like you and me can play that can change what that midnight story looks like. We've already been talking about them all through this chapter. You can be an advocate who does jail ministry, mentors inmates, provides support for their families, speaks up for people inside the jail, and stands beside them in court.

In the next chapter, I'm going to get very specific about what it looks like to step into those roles. This chapter is for you if you've been wondering what you can do. I'm going to break down specific ideas and suggestions for how you can get involved in your community in a way that can create a positive ripple effect that spreads.

PART 4

THE REACH

Restoring Families and Communities

"Bear one another's burdens, and so fulfill the law of Christ."(Galatians 6:2)

CHAPTER 9

Stories of the Redeemed

I've worked around addiction, crime, and recovery long enough to know that real change is never isolated. We like to think of transformation as a personal thing—*my* sobriety, *my* healing, *my* second chance. Individual transformation does matter. But one person's transformation is never the end of the story. No one lives in a vacuum. Every life is connected to another life.

In chapter 3, you learned that when addiction takes hold of a person, the damage doesn't stay contained. It ripples outward into families, marriages, children, churches, workplaces, and entire communities. One person's collapse creates a wake that pulls others under with them.

But the same thing is true in reverse.

When one life is restored, the healing doesn't stop there either. It moves outward. It shows up in repaired relationships, reclaimed purpose, and people who suddenly have hope because they can see what's possible. Redemption creates ripples just as surely as destruction does.

In this chapter, I want to move past abstractions and show you what I mean through the true stories of real men and women whose lives were changed, where the impact didn't stop with the individual.

Through the stories of Jerry, Houston, and Carla, let me show you what one restored, redeemed life can do.

Jerry's Story: From Menace to Mentor

Jerry was in his mid-20s when addiction took hold. Once it did, it reordered everything in his life. His days started with pain. Before his feet ever hit the floor, the question wasn't "What am I going to do today?" It was "How am I going to stop hurting?"

"The second that I woke up and before my feet hit the ground, my plans for the day were to find something that would keep my body from hurting and to get me high for the day," he told me. That became his full-time job.

He spent his days crawling under strangers' porches, trying to steal Wi-Fi just so he could reach someone—anyone—who might be able to help him get high. Sometimes he'd stay there for an hour. Sometimes four. Sometimes longer. He wouldn't leave until he knew the day was covered. That's how narrow his world had become.

The hardest part of Jerry's story isn't what addiction did to him. It's what it did to the people who loved him. Jerry was a mama's boy in the purest sense. He adored his mother, and she adored him. When she got sick with stage three cancer and went through years of treatment, Jerry was the one sitting beside her. They were close in a way that made others jealous.

That's what makes this next part so painful.

When his mother was dying in hospice, Jerry would wait for her to fall asleep, then take the pain medication she needed to survive the day. When she woke up in pain and cried, begging him to get help, he lied to her. Guilt and shame had swallowed him whole.

Addiction had taken the man who once protected her and turned him into someone she was trying to protect from himself.

There came a moment when Jerry hit rock bottom. At six feet tall, he weighed just 113 pounds and had yellowed skin and visible ribs. He had been awake for days. Starving, he walked three miles in the rain to steal a 50 cent pack of crackers just to survive another day. Unsuccessful, he turned around empty-handed and walked three miles back.

When he got home, soaked and shaking, he prayed a prayer that changed everything. "God, I know you're real. I just want to know if I'm loved enough for You to send me a miracle."

Not long after that, his sister pulled up with groceries. Then someone else showed up. And then someone else. They didn't lecture, condemn, or make demands. They loved him and fed him. As they worked to get his electricity turned back on, they asked him if he wanted help.

He said yes.

They called 23 rehabs, trying to find a place that would take Jerry. He had no money, no insurance, and was in the middle of detoxing. Everyone turned him away. They almost lost hope. Then one place asked when they could get him there.

Detoxing at treatment was brutal, but he did it. As he got clean, he started rebuilding himself. He learned structure and took responsibility for his actions. He set new priorities and leaned into his faith. As he remembered how to live again, something unexpected happened.

The people he had hurt, betrayed, and stolen from started calling Jerry to say they were proud of him. That's when he realized this wasn't only about surviving. He was on a path to redemption, and he wasn't walking it alone.

Eventually, Jerry came back to the very community he once devastated. He walked back into a church he had avoided out of shame and instead of rejection, he found restoration.

Today, Jerry is focused on others. He's sober, grounded, and working in a ministry that leads others out of the same darkness he once lived in. His past didn't disqualify him. It equipped him.

Jerry's life is proof that one man's transformation doesn't end with him. It reaches backward into broken families and forward into futures that once felt impossible. He didn't just get his life back for himself. He got it back so he could give it away.

Not every road into addiction looks the same, and not every path out begins at the same place. Some stories start not with physical pain, but with emotional wounds so deep they reshape a person long before drugs ever enter the picture. Jerry's story shows how trauma can hollow a person out and lead them to try to fill the void with substances. But it also illustrates how honesty, accountability, and grace can rebuild a person from the inside out.

Houston's Story: Full-Throttle Transformation

Houston has always lived at one hundred miles per hour. That's just who he is. With Houston, the question was never how fast he was going. He was always going fast. The question was which direction. When he was running from God, he did it at full throttle. When he turned toward Him, he did that the same way too.

Everyone knew Houston. He was the life of the party and the guy you wanted to be around because you knew he'd make the night unforgettable. He's funny, fearless, wild, and there's almost nothing he won't do. Wherever he goes, he's a presence. He fills the room.

Today, those are great qualities. But back then, those qualities put him and those around him on a slippery slope. When someone like Houston spirals, he doesn't spiral alone. Houston pulled people with him as he went, and he always had to take things one step further.

Eventually, some serious trouble caught up with him. After multiple arrests and a string of escalating charges, Houston was staring down real prison sentences. By that point, the district attorney's office had had its fill. From their perspective, Houston was a lost cause, and they were ready to wash their hands of him.

That's when two men stepped in. One was my law partner at the time (now circuit judge), Shawn Fry. The other was my friend, Pastor Tim McLauchlin.

Pastor McLauchlin had gotten to know Houston in jail. Instead of seeing a lost cause, he saw an opportunity. Somehow, he got through to Houston and helped him see that if he was ever going to change, it had to be now.

Pastor McLauchlin reached out to Shawn and asked if there was any way to redirect Houston's path. Could they trade a dead-end sentence for a drug treatment center and a real chance at transformation?

Figuring it out took time. The DA's office wasn't that receptive to the idea at first, but they kept pushing. After all, what did they have to lose? If drug treatment didn't work, Houston would just go back to prison. Eventually, the DA's office agreed to take a chance. He was furloughed to an out-of-state program instead of going straight to serve his sentence.

Although Houston wasn't my client, he was someone I knew of. I watched the case unfold, and then he disappeared, like people sometimes do when they go far away for treatment. At the time, I didn't know much about recovery. I hoped he was doing well. A year or two went by. I hadn't seen a violation come across my desk, so I figured maybe it had worked for him.

And then, one day, I walked into White County Court, and sitting in the front row of the gallery was Houston.

He looked good. Of course, he was still the same Houston, moving at a hundred miles a minute, even when sitting still. He spotted me immediately. "Brett?! Brett!"

I walked over and asked the obvious question, "What are you doing here? Are you in trouble?"

He laughed. "No, no. I graduated. I'm working with a treatment program now. I'm here helping get someone else into the program."

That's when it hit me. Houston didn't just survive. He turned around and ran straight back to the front lines.

For the next year or two, I saw him in court all the time. If he wasn't in court, he was calling me on the phone. "I know you've got some swings in you, Brett," he would say. "Can you help us?" He spent his days drafting letters, arranging furloughs, talking to judges, and helping men and women get a chance just like he had been given. There's an old truth in recovery that one of the best ways to stay free is to help free someone else. Houston lived that out immediately.

Then, one day, I didn't see him anymore, and that worried me.

I later learned that when he'd disappeared, he'd actually gone and become a pastor. He started pastoring a growing church, and he stayed in the fight. We stayed connected, and over time, we got to know each other more personally because we were both pastoring and speaking at the same events.

Today, we have a standing Friday lunch at our favorite local café as often as we can. When we sit down to eat, we can barely finish a bite because if someone doesn't know me, they know him. Someone is always coming up to the table. Houston is one of *those* figures in the community now.

And get this—he married a pharmacist. That still makes me laugh, because only Houston could get sober, get married, and then open a pharmacy with his wife.

Most importantly, Houston never left the battle. From the moment he was pulled off the field and healed, he went right back in. Still going the same speed, but in the opposite direction.

Houston's story is loud in the best way. You can see his transformation from a distance through his leadership and in the way an entire community now leans on him. His life shows what happens when restoration is trusted with weight and carried forward at full speed.

But not every collapse is public, and not every rescue begins in handcuffs or courtrooms. Some battles are fought behind a smile. Some addictions grow quietly behind good manners, bright futures, and a life that looks "just fine." Carla's story reminds us that what we see is not always what's true. Sometimes the most dramatic transformations begin when the mask finally falls.

Carla's Story: When the Mask Fell

I met Carla* the way you meet a lot of people in a small community—over coffee and pancakes.

There's a little diner near our house that's been a hub in our area for years. For a long stretch of my life, I ate breakfast there Tuesday through Friday with the same group of men. Donna and I ate there for dinner plenty of nights too. When you frequent the same place long enough, you don't just learn the menu; you also learn the people. Carla was one of those people.

Carla was 16 when she started waitressing there. From the beginning, she had that rare warmth some people carry. She was bright, cheerful, and friendly…the kind of young woman people naturally gravitated toward. She would talk with Donna and me when her shift slowed down about school, plans after graduation, and the future. We've raised five kids, so we're always in "parent mode" by default. We cared about Carla and expected good things for her.

And honestly? Carla looked like she had it all together.

She was sweet, polished, and beautiful in a way that makes you think, *she's going to be just fine.* She came from a family I knew well. They were hardworking and visible in the community. Her dad was active in church life, the kind of cowboy preacher you'll see at rodeos and horse events giving the devotional before things get started. Carla's life, from the outside, looked steady.

Then something shifted.

First, it was subtle. She went through a breakup, and her smile slipped a little. She started looking more worn down, more frazzled, and less like the girl we'd known. I chalked it up to heartbreak. A lot of young people go through that season where life starts to hurt for the first time and you're just trying to find your footing again.

But it didn't get better. It got worse. She quit working at the diner, and the whole community started wondering what in the world was going on with Carla.

The next time I saw her dad, I asked him directly. I'll never forget how his face changed. He broke down and said, "It's bad. I can't get her back." He'd been watching his child disappear right before his eyes, and he didn't know what to do.

I then learned that Carla had gotten hooked on drugs. The once bright and shining young woman was now caught in an addiction that was destroying her life. Carla's own words explain it better than I ever could.

"I was very focused on trying to paint a pretty picture for the outside world," she said. "There was a void that I had that only Jesus could fill. I was not filling that void with Jesus, so it led me down the destructive path of using drugs and alcohol."

Carla was around 12 the first time she stole wine from her mother's fridge to quiet her mind enough to sleep. After years of keeping her real pain hidden, the mask she'd been wearing got heavier and heavier. She wanted to be liked, to fit in, and make the "right choices" so people would approve of her life. Then she got into a crowd where drugs were normal. Prescription pain medication started showing up. She wasn't raised around that, but it looked like fun. It looked like something you did on the weekend just because.

By 17, she used her first prescription pill. Within a week, she knew she couldn't function without it. Within six months it escalated. That's the thing about addiction: It lies to you at the beginning. It makes poison look harmless. She convinced herself that she was okay because she was able to keep up a normal-looking life from outward appearances.

She went to college, worked full-time, and was even promoted to manager at her new job. *Everything's going good,* she told herself. *I'm in school, I'm working, I'm functioning.* But inside, Carla was detaching from relationships, isolating, and living another life in secret.

"I fell in love with the drugs so much that it was all that I had cared about," she said. "Being alive meant less than actually being high. It became the center of my life, and it took everything. It stole everything from me."

She overdosed, and her mask fell off in front of everyone. There was no hiding it anymore. Her doctor suggested she try church, but Carla didn't think God wanted to hear from someone like her anymore. God was mad at her, and she couldn't imagine Jesus would want a relationship with a girl who had made those choices.

Addiction makes those lies believable.

"I got to a point using drugs that I wouldn't look in the mirror anymore," she said. "I didn't want to see who I had become because I knew I had a grandmother who prayed for me as a child and other family members as well."

The addiction got more dangerous when Carla started using fentanyl pills. After another overdose, she overheard a doctor telling her mother she needed Narcan everywhere—at home, in the car, in drawers—because overdoses were going to keep happening if she didn't get clean.

That was the wake-up call.

Within days, a door opened into long-term treatment. Here's something Carla said that I've learned to emphasize to people: God may open the door, but you still have to step through it. He opened the way, and she walked in.

Carla spent a little over a year in the program. She said she would do it all over again because it's where she learned who Jesus really is—a living Savior who wants a relationship and brings deliverance.

My wife and I were there when Carla graduated from treatment. Donna leaned over and said, "I have never seen her look more beautiful."

She was right. Carla wasn't just sober. She was whole.

Then Carla did something I still love telling people about because it's the kind of thing only God would think to do. She entered a fair pageant. She had never even attended a pageant before, but she wanted to step out in confidence and prayed, "Lord, if this is a door You want me to walk through, open it and keep it open."

He did. Carla won. If you've never been to a pageant, you might not realize how public they are. When they placed the crown on her head, she wasn't in a private room. She was on stage in front of the same community where she hadn't set a good example not that long ago.

That's what stopped me in my tracks. Because what I saw at that moment wasn't a pageant. What I saw was God rebuilding someone in front of everybody.

I think Carla said it best herself. "Look what He can do when you let Him."

Today, Carla's sharing the truth and her testimony in churches. Carla's story is a reminder that addiction doesn't always start in the gutter. Sometimes it starts behind a smile and a pretty face. But when the mask falls, it doesn't have to be the end.

It can be the beginning.

The Ripple Keeps Moving

If you step back and look at these stories together, a pattern starts to emerge.

Jerry's life shows us what happens when a man who once took from everyone around him learns how to give his life away instead. His healing didn't just save him; it restored family bonds and created a pathway for others to follow.

Houston's story proves that when someone restored is trusted with responsibility, the impact can scale. Leadership, influence, and community impact don't come from perfection. They come from obedience, consistency, and staying in the fight.

Carla's story shows us something equally important. Not every collapse is obvious. Some addictions grow behind external appearances, potential, and lives that look "fine" from the outside. Her redemption reminds us that when the mask falls, it doesn't have to be the end. Sometimes it's the moment everything finally begins.

Different paths. Different wounds. Different outcomes. Same truth.

When one life changes, others are affected. Families heal, communities shift, and hope spreads. The ripple keeps moving.

That's why this work matters. Does every story end perfectly? No. But restoration is contagious. It gives people permission to believe that their past doesn't have to dictate their future. One life is never just one life. That's exactly why redemption is worth fighting for.

It's going to take more than one person at a time to make a dent in the need for addiction recovery. The justice system can't—and shouldn't—do it alone. It's time for the Church to step forward and join the fight.

CHAPTER 10

The Call of the Church

Once upon a time, there was a king who gathered all of his subjects for a great banquet at his castle. He'd spent many days preparing for the banquet, setting up two rows of tables decorated with the finest china and flatware. As the guests filed into the castle, the smell of the delicious food that his chefs had prepared filled the air.

A servant met each guest as they passed through the main doorway of the banquet hall. He silently directed them individually either to the table on the left or the table on the right. This caused a bit of confusion for a moment. There didn't seem to be any rhyme or reason for the seating arrangement. Family members weren't always seated together, and rich and poor were intermingled at the tables.

There was some murmuring, but since each place setting was equally beautiful, no one complained for long. After all, he was the king. He could do as he wished. Finally, everyone was seated, and the king strode through the dining hall to take his place at the head of the room. The room fell silent in anticipation.

The king raised his arms in welcome. "My friends," he said. "Thank you for coming to join me tonight. I'm very pleased to have you here. But before we begin, I want to give special thanks to a group of you."

The guests on the left side of the room straightened in their seats. Now we're getting to it, they thought. We're about to get the recognition we deserve. You see, seated at the king's left were many important members of the kingdom. They had built businesses, grown families, and become people of some prominence. Many had given great sums of money to this or that endeavor and enjoyed the recognition that came when their generosity was recognized.

But to everyone's surprise, the king turned and addressed those seated at his right.

"My friends," he said with a smile. "You are the guests of honor tonight. I have spent years preparing this feast for you. Tonight, I am announcing that everything I have in my kingdom is yours! Because you're the kind of people who fed me when I was hungry. And when I was thirsty, you gave me something to drink. When I was lonely, you invited me into your homes. And when I needed warm clothing or got sick, you made sure I was taken care of. You didn't turn your backs on me when I was in prison, either, but instead came to visit me."

Guests at both tables began whispering back and forth to each other. Those on the left were indignant.

"What is he talking about? How could the king give his kingdom to them and ignore us?"

"Surely he's gotten us mixed up. We've done so much more than those others. And what does he mean? He's never been hungry or thirsty or in jail."

Meanwhile, those on the king's right were surprised and, honestly, confused. They had been happy just to be in the king's presence tonight. They hadn't come for accolades, and they had no idea what the king was talking about. When had they done any of these things he claimed they'd done? Finally, a man seated near the end of the table where the king stood respectfully rose from his seat.

"Yes, my friend," the king said kindly. "What is it? Speak freely."

The man cleared his throat and began, "Forgive me, my king, but although certainly we all would be willing to serve you in whatever ways you need, none of us remember doing any of the things you just mentioned."

Many heads on the king's right nodded in humility as the man spoke. On the left, men and women snickered behind their hands and elbowed each other. Surely the king would see his mistake and honor their own table, as they deserved.

"You're the king," the man continued. "We've never seen you hungry or thirsty, or without clothes to wear, or in prison."

The king smiled gently. "No," he replied. "You haven't seen me in need, but you have seen and helped others in my kingdom. And anytime you helped even the youngest, weakest, or most pitiful of my people, it's like you were helping me. That's exactly the kind of person who belongs here with me in my kingdom."

Then, face turning stern, he turned to the people on the left. "As for all of you…you've never helped anyone but yourselves. You aren't fit to be members of my kingdom. You've shown your true colors in the way you ignore and oppress those in need. That's not the kind of kingdom I run around here. You can see yourselves out."

The Mandate

There's a temptation, especially in church circles, to minister to hurting people as an optional activity. We act like only super-spiritual churches, pastors, and volunteers who feel called to deal with messy people and hard situations are responsible for taking action.

But that's not what Jesus says. You probably caught on that the story at the beginning of this chapter is a mirror of the passage in Matthew 25 where Jesus talks about feeding the hungry, visiting the prisoner, and caring for the sick. Notice what the passage says:

> Then the King will say to those on his right, "Come, you who are blessed by my Father; take your inheritance, the kingdom prepared for you since the creation of the world. For I was hungry and you gave Me something to eat, I was thirsty and you gave Me something to drink, I was a stranger and you invited Me in, I needed clothes and you clothed Me, I was sick and you looked after Me, I was in prison and you came to visit Me."
>
> Then the righteous will answer him, "Lord, when did we see You hungry and feed You, or thirsty and give You

something to drink? When did we see You a stranger and invite You in, or needing clothes and clothe You? When did we see You sick or in prison and go to visit You?"

The King will reply, "Truly I tell you, whatever you did for one of the least of these brothers and sisters of mine, you did for Me."

Then He will say to those on His left, "Depart from Me, you who are cursed, into the eternal fire prepared for the devil and his angels. For I was hungry and you gave Me nothing to eat, I was thirsty and you gave Me nothing to drink, I was a stranger and you did not invite Me in, I needed clothes and you did not clothe Me, I was sick and in prison and you did not look after Me."

They also will answer, "Lord, when did we see You hungry or thirsty or a stranger or needing clothes or sick or in prison, and did not help You?"

He will reply, "Truly I tell you, whatever you did not do for one of the least of these, you did not do for Me." (Matt 25:34–45, NIV)

Notice how Jesus doesn't frame caring for others as a suggestion. He doesn't present it as a side ministry or an optional outreach for churches that are "ready" for it. He presents it as a dividing line.

That should get our attention.

Helping others isn't about doing more good works or checking another box. It's about *obedience*. The words Jesus uses in

Matthew 25 aren't symbolic or exaggerated for effect. This is Jesus telling people what it looks like to belong to His kingdom.

I don't want you to think I'm scolding the Church. But I do want to call back to what the Church has always been at its best—the hands and feet of Jesus.

The Gospel was never meant to be preached from a distance. Jesus didn't shout instructions from the safe side of suffering. He stepped into it and touched lepers and ate with sinners. He spoke dignity into people everyone else had written off, and He told His followers to do the same.

But it's very easy to take the attitude that addiction and incarceration are problems "out there." Not so. The truth is, addiction and incarceration are already sitting in our pews. If a church has 40 people in attendance, odds are at least four of them are directly impacted by addiction personally through a spouse, a child, a sibling, or a parent. They may not raise their hand to admit it when they show up looking fine on Sunday morning, but they're carrying it.

Ignoring that reality doesn't protect the Church. It weakens it. Pretending this work belongs to someone else doesn't make us neutral. It makes us absent. The mandate is clear. Every follower of Christ is called to be a minister of the Gospel in someone else's life. The only question is whether we're willing to respond.

When the Church Becomes a Club

There's a quiet shift that can happen over time inside any church if we're not paying attention. It doesn't start with bad intentions. In fact, most of the time it starts with good ones.

When people come to church, they often find community, safety, and belonging. But spend too long focusing inward and slowly, almost imperceptibly, the church stops being a mission and starts becoming a club.

Clubs exist to serve their members. They protect comfort, reinforce sameness, and reward those who already know the rules. Clubs aren't necessarily hostile to outsiders, they're just not built for them. And that's where things get dangerous.

The people Jesus keeps pointing us toward—the addicted, the incarcerated, the broken, the ashamed—don't know the rules. They don't dress right or speak church language. They often behave in ways that don't feel predictable or safe. And if a church has quietly become a club, those people feel it the moment they walk through the door.

No one has to say a word. The hesitation and sideways glances do all the talking. I've seen churches with excellent theology and spotless buildings silently communicate, *You're welcome here…as long as you don't disrupt anything.*

But Jesus never built anything that required the broken to stay quiet. He built a kingdom that advances through interruption.

When churches begin prioritizing order and routine over obedience, comfort over calling, and reputation over redemption, they may still gather, but they stop reaching out. And a church that stops reaching out eventually stops looking like Jesus.

This is where the story Jesus tells in Matthew 25 becomes unsettling. Because the people who missed it weren't openly cruel. They weren't villains. They were just busy. They were focused inward on their own lives and building their own pet project. They were convinced that faith was about what happened *inside* their circle.

Jesus's response is sobering. "You ignored the people I sent to you. I don't know you."

You don't have to reject Christ to miss Him. You just have to overlook the people He keeps showing up as.

The church was never meant to be a protected space for the already whole. It was meant to be a hospital, a refuge, and a launch point, and all of those places are messy. So the question isn't whether broken people belong in church. It's whether the church remembers that it exists, in large part, for the broken.

The Real Battle

If the church becoming a club were only a cultural problem, it would be easier to fix. We could tweak programs, rewrite mission statements, or schedule more outreach events. But that's not where the real battle is. The real battle is the slow drift of the human heart toward self-protection. We want to be comfortable and in control. We love the familiar.

Left unchecked, even people who genuinely love God will begin arranging their faith around what feels safest instead of what's most faithful. We don't wake up one morning deciding to ignore those who are hurting. We just get very good at staying busy with things that don't require sacrifice.

Jesus never framed the battle as "the church versus the world." He framed it as a daily choice between obedience and self-interest, and between love that costs something and love that stays theoretical. Ultimately this isn't about structures, denominations, or leadership styles. It's about whether we're willing to put ourselves second.

Once you truly see the addicted, the incarcerated, the abused, and the discarded, you can't unknow them. You can't pretend their pain isn't real. If you belong to Christ, you can't outsource responsibility forever.

Will we harden ourselves just enough to stay comfortable, or soften ourselves enough to stay obedient?

We make choices one way or the other in small, ordinary moments. We either move toward people who make us uncomfortable, or we quietly step aside. We choose between protecting our images or risking our reputation and seeing interruptions as inconveniences or invitations.

The enemy doesn't need the church to stop believing in Jesus. He just needs us to stop following Him. That's the real battlefield, and the battle is fought long before anyone ever steps into a jail, recovery center, or broken home. It's fought in the private places where we decide what kind of faith we're actually willing to live out.

I challenge you to change the question you're asking yourself from "Should I get involved?" to "How could I *not* get involved?"

Why the Church Must Lead

If the church doesn't step up and lead when it comes to addiction recovery, another institution will. Addiction, incarceration, trauma, and family collapse do not exist in a vacuum. They have to be addressed, but will they be addressed with truth, accountability, and hope? Or with systems that manage damage without restoring people? That would be like using pliers to hammer in a nail, right?

The church was never meant to trail behind culture, reacting after the fact. It was designed to see what others overlook and move first. We must step into places most institutions avoid because when the church leads, it brings something no government agency or nonprofit can replicate: a transformation that affects the heart, not just behavior.

I've watched what happens when the church hesitates. Gaps get filled by bureaucracy, and people get reduced to case numbers. Don't get me wrong—the justice system plays a vital role, but it can't do everything. There's no grace with accountability in the law, and cycles repeat when there's no help for transformation because nothing underneath actually changes.

When the church leads, the pattern breaks. The church understands that people don't just need services, they need belonging. They need rules and restoration, correction and community.

When I say the church needs to lead in this area, I don't mean the church should do everything. But it can set the direction and be the first to say, "We're not waiting for permission to love people who are hard to love."

We can show up early before the crisis becomes a headline. We can stay late after the spotlight moves on, even when the results aren't immediate or measurable. Yes, this kind of leadership is costly. It disrupts comfort, demands humility, and requires courage to stand in places where success doesn't look polished. But it's also the only leadership that lasts.

When the church leads, families stabilize, communities regain trust, and generations change course. The church's calling hasn't changed. We don't lead because it makes us look good. We lead because we're called to love. Silence creates a vacuum, and love refuses to leave it empty.

Becoming the Four Friends

In the Gospel of Mark, a paralyzed man is brought to Jesus by four friends who refuse to let obstacles stop them. When the house where Jesus is speaking is too crowded, they climb onto the roof, tear it open, and lower their friend down at Jesus's feet. It's one of the clearest pictures we have of faith that shows up in action.

What's easy to miss is that Jesus doesn't begin by praising the man on the mat. Scripture says He responds to the faith of the friends. That detail matters because it tells us that someone else's breakthrough can hinge on our willingness to carry them.

The man couldn't get to Jesus on his own. He didn't have the strength, access, or leverage to make it happen. Without those four friends, he would have stayed outside, close enough to hear hope but unable to reach it.

This is where our understanding of change often breaks down. We talk about transformation like it's purely an individual responsibility, but many people don't need another lecture, consequence, or program. They need four friends who are willing to carry weight they didn't create and problems they didn't cause.

Becoming the four friends means accepting that effort is not the same as ability. Someone can want help and still be unable to reach it without assistance. We must decide that another person's paralysis, whether physical, emotional, or spiritual, is not an excuse for our distance.

Those friends didn't debate whether the man deserved help or worry about whether he might end up back on the mat again. They saw the need, picked him up, and moved. That's the reaction we need to have as the Church because it's important to note that they worked together. No one person could have carried him alone, and no one person receives individual credit in the story. The burden was shared, and so was the faith.

Sometimes the greatest act of faith isn't believing that God can heal. It's believing that obedience still matters even when healing hasn't happened yet. The roof-tearing faith comes before the miracle, not after it. Is tearing off a roof disruptive? Yes. It damages property, breaks social expectations, and makes religious people uncomfortable. But Jesus didn't stop the four friends or correct their methods. He honored them.

When the Church becomes the four friends, everything changes. "What would it take to carry them there?" becomes the focus that moves faith out of theory and into responsibility. That's how lives get to Jesus.

But it's one thing to say, "Yes, we're in!" and another to know how to start. In the next chapter, I'm going to break down exactly what it takes to start an addiction and recovery ministry as a church.

CHAPTER 11

Starting a Ministry

Saying yes to the call to help in addiction recovery is a powerful moment. But responding to the call takes more than willingness. At some point, good intentions have to turn into something people can actually step into.

This is where a lot of churches stall. They know recovery matters. They want to help, but they're unsure where to begin, what's safe, what's wise, and what's sustainable. The gap between compassion and action can feel overwhelming without a roadmap.

Recovery ministry starts with clarity about what the church is called to do, what it isn't, and how to enter this work without burning people out or doing harm along the way. You now know why the church must engage. In this chapter, I'm going to explain *how* to begin an addiction recovery ministry in real, workable steps.

Step 1: Understand Addiction and Become Trauma-Informed

The first step to ministering to people in or recovering from addiction is to become trauma-informed.

You can't help what you don't understand, and nowhere is that truer than in recovery work. Many of the people who walk through the doors of a church carrying addiction are making choices in response to their pain. It may look like they're living in purposeful defiance against God, but they're often just trying to survive.

Addiction is rooted in trauma far more often than most churches realize. Abuse, neglect, abandonment, violence, and chronic instability reshape how people see authority, relationships, and safety. If we don't understand that, we end up misreading behavior and responding in ways that push people further away instead of drawing them in.

Trauma affects how people trust, how they make decisions, and how they react under stress. It can look like resisting authority, behaving inconsistently, or being emotionally volatile. Those responses were learned in environments where survival mattered more than rules. When churches mistake trauma responses for spiritual failure, they unintentionally reinforce the very patterns they're trying to break.

Becoming trauma-informed doesn't mean excusing harmful behavior or removing accountability. It means knowing *why* someone responds the way they do so you can apply accountability wisely and with clarity.

Whenever possible, churches should take advantage of trauma-informed training offered by state agencies or nonprofit organizations. These resources exist in many communities and can give leaders a shared language and framework before they ever engage directly in recovery ministry. Training helps teams respond consistently instead of emotionally.

If those resources aren't available locally, look for other churches that are already doing the work well and ask to learn from them. You can also bring in someone who can teach your leadership team and volunteers.

Recovery ministry doesn't require perfection, but it does require the willingness to admit we don't know everything and the discipline to learn before we act.

Step 2: Build a Strategy Before You Enter the Trenches

Good intentions without strategy don't change lives. It burns people out. I've seen churches rush into recovery ministry with big hearts and no plan, only to end up discouraged, overwhelmed, and unsure about what went wrong. Passion is essential, but without direction, it becomes unsustainable.

Every ministry in a church requires a strategy, and recovery ministry is no different. You wouldn't start a children's program, a missions effort, or a building project without clarity on roles, resources, and purpose. Walking into addiction recovery without a plan is like entering a battlefield without knowing where the front lines are drawn.

Ministry, especially ministry when you're in the trenches with those you're serving, demands more than compassion. It requires foresight. You need to know who is responsible for what, where boundaries exist, and how decisions will be made before pressure hits. When chaos shows up—and it will—

clarity is what keeps people from reacting emotionally instead of acting wisely.

Before you launch anything outward, start by teaching the biblical *why*. Members need to understand that this work isn't a trend, a side project, or a response to a crisis. Explain how this work is central to the Gospel. When the why is clear, the what makes sense. This makes it easier to keep going, even when it gets hard.

That's why it's important to prepare the congregation with teaching and guidance from God's Word before asking them to participate. Recovery ministry reshapes a church's culture, not just its calendar. When people know what they're being invited into and why it matters, they step in with open eyes instead of hesitation or fear.

Step 3: Raise an Army

The war against addiction will be won by numbers and unity. The Lone Ranger approach doesn't work in recovery ministry because addiction is never a one-on-one fight. It's layered, relentless, and communal, which means the response must be the same.

Addiction is fought best by an organized, trained, and equipped force. When people rush in without roles, direction, or accountability, good intentions turn into chaos. But when a church moves together with clarity and purpose, it becomes steady, effective, and hard to stop.

This is how momentum builds—as an army advancing with purpose. The rallying cry stays simple and relentless: "Give me one more, Lord."

A healthy recovery ministry requires a team with clearly defined roles. Not everyone needs to do everything, but everyone needs to know where they fit. When people understand their lane, they can serve with confidence instead of confusion. There are a number of roles every recovery ministry will need filled.

> **Supporters.** Some team members are called to meet people where they are. These are listeners and encouragers. They can sit with the addicted without fixing, hear painful stories without flinching, and build trust over time. They walk with individuals and families in crisis, offering steady presence when life feels unstable and overwhelming.
>
> **Logistics.** Others are equipped to help get people where they're going. These advocates understand treatment options, application processes, program rules, and key contacts. They guide people step by step into help, cutting through confusion at moments when clarity feels impossible.
>
> **Providers.** Every strong team also includes people focused on immediate care. Addiction often strips people of basics like clothing, food, transportation, and even a Bible. Meeting those practical needs is stabilizing, and it often opens the door for deeper transformation.

Intercessors. Some of the most important work will be done behind the scenes by prayer warriors who commit to covering the work in prayer.

Restorers and Reintegrators. Finally, recovery ministry must include those committed to restoration and reintegration. These are the bridge builders who help returning individuals find community, housing, work, and discipleship. They ensure that recovery doesn't end at sobriety and leads people back into church life and society with dignity and purpose.

Some of the strongest soldiers in this fight are the ones who've already been through it. Recovered men and women, along with their families, bring credibility, empathy, and hope that can't be taught in a classroom. They know the terrain because they survived it.

When the right team is in place, no one carries the full weight alone. No one falls through the cracks.

Step 4: Set Clear, Loving Boundaries

Boundaries will protect your ministry. Without clear boundaries, churches become more vulnerable to burnout, confusion, and unintended harm. When expectations are undefined, good intentions quickly turn into exhaustion, and resentment can start to form.

Set healthy boundaries *before* the crisis shows up. Churches need to determine in advance how much money they are willing to spend, how much time volunteers are expected to give, and what safety guidelines must be followed. They also need clarity on who is qualified to serve, in what roles, and at what stage of recovery.

Setting boundaries in these areas is good stewardship. Addiction often comes with chaos, and chaos can break down places without structure. Clear limits prevent manipulation, protect volunteers, and ensure the mission remains focused on long-term transformation rather than short-term crisis management.

One of the hardest truths churches must embrace is that "come as you are" does not mean "serve as you are." Everyone is welcome to receive help, grace, and care, but leadership and service require readiness, stability, and accountability. Love opens the door, but wisdom decides when a person is safe to serve. When an addicted individual has experienced freedom and transformation, they're often eager to dive in and start serving. This is admirable, but not always wise.

Saying no or not yet is often an act of love. When boundaries are clear and consistent, they create safety for everyone involved and allow ministry to last longer than a moment of emotion.

Step 5: Communicate and Prepare the Congregation

Culture is never accidental in a church. What's celebrated from the pulpit becomes normal in the pews, and what's ignored quietly becomes avoided. If recovery ministry is going to take root, the entire congregation has to understand what it is, why it matters, and what it will look like in real life.

That means leaders must talk openly about recovery, healing, and transformation. Addiction can't remain a whispered topic or a side conversation handled only in private offices. When pastors normalize these stories by naming them, praying for them, and teaching about them, the church learns that redemption is not an exception to the Gospel. It *is* the Gospel.

One of the most powerful things a church can do is celebrate people coming out of treatment publicly and joyfully in a way that says, "We see you, and we're glad you're here." When leaders show visible excitement over restoration, the congregation takes its cues and follows their lead.

This kind of culture doesn't happen through announcements alone. It's built through repetition and example. Teach the vision. Demonstrate it through leadership. Then invite the church to live it out together, one restored life at a time.

Step 6: Make the Ministry Visible and Safe

People who are hurting rarely ask first if a place is safe. They watch to see if it *feels* safe. Long before someone raises their hand or walks forward, they're listening to the language, noticing the tone, and paying attention to what the church is doing. Safety is often communicated quietly, but it's always communicated clearly, whether done intentionally or not. Choose to be intentional.

If recovery ministry matters, it needs to be seen. That means mentioning it in announcements, reflecting it in signage, and reinforcing it through language from the pulpit. When recovery is spoken about naturally and respectfully, it signals that people don't have to hide or explain themselves to belong.

First-time visitors should leave knowing the ministry is a place where healing is understood and welcomed. They may not be ready to ask for help yet, but they should know where to turn when they are ready. Visibility removes guesswork and lowers the risk of rejection.

Programs matter, but atmosphere speaks first. A church's posture toward brokenness is felt long before it's explained, and when safety is evident, people begin to believe that restoration might be possible for them too.

Step 7: Be Ready for People to Come in "Hot"

People coming out of faith-based recovery don't arrive cautious or half-interested. They arrive hungry. When someone has just experienced freedom, forgiveness, and clarity for the first time, they're often spiritually on fire and eager to run headfirst into everything the church represents.

That kind of passion is a gift, but it needs direction. What these individuals need most in this season is structure, steady discipleship, and real community. They don't need to be put on display or fast-tracked into responsibility. They need room to grow roots before they're asked to bear weight.

Without intentional engagement, that fire can cool off just as quickly as it ignited. Confusion, isolation, or unrealistic expectations can undo momentum if no one is walking alongside them. Early recovery is a fragile and formative season, and what happens during that time matters.

The church must be ready to disciple without rushing. Healthy ministry protects passion while guiding it patiently, understanding that long-term faithfulness is built through consistency, not urgency.

The church also has to be willing to welcome people who don't look like us, smell like us, or dress like us. Recovery doesn't arrive polished, and transformation rarely shows up tidy. If we're only comfortable with people once they look "church ready," then we've misunderstood who the church is for.

I remember a man who started coming to church who smelled so bad you noticed him before you saw him. He hadn't showered in days, maybe longer. *Man, he stinks!* I thought to myself. But the next thought I had checked my attitude at the door. *He doesn't smell that way to Jesus.* Immediately, I stopped noticing the smell, and I went on to have a quality conversation with the man.

That was the last time I saw that man. I learned that he had a stroke two weeks later and died. I'm so grateful for that conversation with him because, honestly, how he smelled was the least important thing about him. If I had decided that his presence was too uncomfortable for me to be around, I would have missed an interaction God wanted me to have.

Jesus ignored our spiritual stench, and He calls us to do the same for others. Grace opens the door wide and says, "You belong here." It doesn't flinch at mess or recoil from brokenness.

But grace never stops at welcome. Real grace leads toward truth, and truth leads toward change. That man didn't stay where he was forever—and neither should we expect anyone to. Love meets people where they are and then walks with them forward, patiently and faithfully, toward the life God has for them.

The Invitation

The movie *Hacksaw Ridge*[17] made a big impression on me. It is a World War II film about Desmond Doss, a US Army medic who refused to carry a weapon because of his faith. He served on the front lines and is credited with saving 75 wounded soldiers during one of the war's bloodiest battles without firing a single shot.

In the film, every time Doss dragged one wounded and injured soldier to safety, he prayed that God would allow him to save one more.

That should be our prayer, too, but as individuals, we can't do it alone. This work was never meant to rest on one set of shoulders. No pastor, judge, volunteer, or church can carry the weight of addiction and recovery alone. The call is not to single out a few willing people, but to call leaders up into shared responsibility and shared vision.

Unity across the Church is not optional in this fight. Addiction doesn't respect denominational lines, budgets, or job titles, so the response can't either. When churches work in isolation, they exhaust themselves. When they move together, they become resilient.

---

[17] *Hacksaw Ridge*, directed by Mel Gibson (Santa Monica, CA: Summit Entertainment, 2016), DVD or streaming.

It's important to name this for what it is. To fight addiction is to fight spiritual warfare. Lives, families, and futures are on the line, and the enemy doesn't retreat easily. We need an army.

The question isn't whether addiction exists in your community. It does. Is your church ready to become a place that helps raise an army of people who are willing to stand their ground? Is it willing to fight back against addiction, and keep asking God, "Give me one more"?

Want Help?

If your church is feeling the pull to step into this work, you don't have to figure it out alone. I've walked this road from the courtroom to the church pew, from crisis response to long-term recovery. I've seen what works and what doesn't, and I've walked with a number of churches as they launch recovery ministries.

If you'd like help getting started building a recovery ministry that's both compassionate and sustainable, I'm willing to come alongside you. The need is real. The harvest is ready. If your church is ready to join the fight, I'd be honored to help you start. For more information on how to schedule me to speak and/or train your ministry team, visit https://BrettKnight.com/book.

PART 5

THE RESPONSE

Becoming the Solution

"Therefore if the Son makes you free, you shall be free indeed."
(John 8:36)

CHAPTER 12

How to Heal What Punishment Can't

For most of this book, I've been talking about systems like the courts, churches, communities, and families. I've been addressing the places where decisions get made and policies get written because those environments shape lives for better or for worse.

But eventually, every system runs into the same wall. You can arrest someone, sentence them, discipline them, supervise them, and even rehabilitate them, and still feel the quiet frustration of asking, "Why isn't this working?" Consequences may interrupt behavior, but they don't answer the deeper question underneath it.

I've spent years watching people cycle through punishment, jail, probation, treatment, relapse, and shame. What I've learned—sometimes painfully—is that punishment can control actions for a season, but it cannot heal a wound. It can restrain, but it cannot restore.

So what actually *changes* a person? What creates transformation that goes beyond temporarily staying out of trouble or "being good"? That's what this chapter is about.

This chapter marks a shift. We're moving from talking about institutions to talking about individuals. Although systems manage brokenness, what people really need is soul-level healing that restores wholeness. This kind of healing is the root of defeating addiction. If we don't address it, we'll just keep building punishments for wounds that were never meant to be punished in the first place.

What Kind of Healing Are We Actually Talking About?

When we talk about healing in this book, we're not talking about behavior management or surface-level improvement. We're talking about something deeper that the Scripture has always pointed to but we often overlook. The original Greek word in the Bible is *sozo*.

Sozo is a Greek word that shows up all throughout the New Testament, and it's far richer than how we usually translate it. It means to save, to rescue, to deliver, to heal, and to make whole. Sozo encompasses not just one of those things, but all of them together. It's whole-person rescue, not partial relief.

You see this clearly in Matthew 9, in the story of the woman with the issue of blood. After she reaches out and touches Jesus's garment, He tells her, "Your faith has saved you." The word He uses there for "saved" is sozo. He wasn't just saying her bleeding stopped. He was saying something much bigger had happened. Her body, her dignity, her identity, and her place in the community were being restored.

You see it again in Acts 16:31, when Paul tells the jailer, "Believe in the Lord Jesus, and you will be saved..." The word saved here is also sozo. It wasn't a promise of a momentary decision or a future destination. It was an invitation into a transformed life that is rescued, healed, and made whole.

This matters because sobriety by itself is not the same thing as restoration. You can stop using substances and still be ruled by fear, anger, shame, or trauma. You can comply with rules and still be deeply broken on the inside. That's partial healing, and partial healing almost always leads people back into old patterns when pressure returns.

Sozo healing is different. It's not a momentary fix or a one-time altar call. It's a lifelong process of becoming whole in spirit, mind, body, and relationships. Truth replaces lies, safety replaces chaos, and love replaces shame. That kind of healing is something punishment has never been able to produce. It's a beautiful thing to behold.

What Healing Looks Like in Real Life

When real healing takes place, it doesn't stay hidden. You can see it before you ever hear someone explain it. Wholeness leaves evidence in a person's posture, presence, and the way they begin to inhabit their own life again.

Health is often the first outward sign of healing. When people have been healed from addiction, they stand straighter, make eye contact, and carry themselves differently. Their weight stabilizes, energy returns, and the constant tension of survival mode starts to loosen its grip. Emotionally, fear and defensiveness begin to fade, replaced by a growing sense of safety. The person can receive love again instead of holding others at arm's length and constantly bracing for the next hit.

Next comes trust, which may be the most fragile and meaningful change of all. The frantic pace of the addicted mind begins to slow down. Manipulation gives way to honest communication because they no longer feel like honesty is dangerous. For the first time in a long while, real relationships start to form, and these relationships aren't transactional, strategic, or rooted in fear of abandonment.

From there, confidence begins to take shape. People stop thinking only about getting through today and start imagining a future again. Family relationships that once felt too broken to repair are approached with humility and hope, and the focus slowly shifts outward from "me," to "my family," and eventually to "how can I help someone else?" One of the clearest signs of wholeness is when people who have been rescued develop a deep desire to rescue others.

That's what healing looks like when it's real—a life that's being rebuilt from the inside out and a person who's steady, connected, and moving forward with purpose.

Why Faith-Based Healing Matters

There's an important distinction we have to make if we're going to talk honestly about healing. Justice exists to make things right, while grace exists to make people whole. Both matter, but they are not the same thing, and they do not produce the same results when it comes to broken lives.

Isn't all treatment basically the same? I hear this objection all the time. After all, structure is structure, rules are rules, and accountability is accountability…right? While those things can help stabilize behavior for a season, they don't touch the deeper question of why someone became an addict in the first place.

Sobriety alone is not the same as healing. You can remove substances, enforce compliance, and still leave a person trapped in fear, shame, and isolation. Without addressing the soul, the best you can hope for is behavior management, and behavior management always breaks down under pressure.

Faith-based recovery is different because it aims for sozo, not just behavior control. It doesn't stop at getting someone clean. It presses toward restoration, identity, forgiveness, and wholeness. It acknowledges that something inside a person must be healed, not just restrained.

At the center of that kind of healing is Christ Himself. Willpower can create short-term change, and structure can provide temporary stability, but neither can redeem a heart or make someone new. As described in 2 Corinthians 5:17 (NKJV): "Therefore, if anyone is **in Christ**, he is a new creation; old things have passed away; behold, all things have become new." Only Jesus heals what punishment never could, and only grace has the power to rebuild a life from the inside out.

Faith-based recovery programs aren't a final destination; they're outposts on the journey to freedom.

Faith-Based Recovery as an Outpost of Grace

Faith-based recovery programs are absolutely necessary part of the journey from addiction to freedom. I've come to see them as modern-day outposts—places you go to survive the battle, get stabilized, and be restored enough to move forward. They provide safety, supply, and structure when someone's life is falling apart.

But an outpost is not a homeland. Recovery programs are not replacements for the church, the family, or the wider community. They exist to rescue and restore, not to isolate people permanently from the world they're meant to reenter.

Graduation from a recovery program is not the finish line. Healing doesn't end when someone completes a program, earns a certificate, or reaches a sobriety milestone. If recovery stops there, we've shifted the environment, but we haven't fulfilled the mission.

The real goal is reintegration. It's helping men and women step back into healthy relationships, meaningful work, a church family, and a life with purpose. Recovery programs rescue them, retool them, and return them to the world. Let's talk about what that looks like day to day.

A Day in the Life of Faith-Based Recovery

Up to this point, we've talked about *why* faith-based recovery matters and *what* kind of healing it's actually aiming for. Healing isn't just a belief system. It's a rhythm, a pattern, a way of living that gets practiced day after day.

That's where faith-based recovery separates itself from models that rely only on crisis intervention or behavior management. It removes chaos and replaces it with structure that trains the heart, the mind, and the spirit at the same time. To understand why it works, you have to look at what life actually looks like inside it, as told by my friend Brandi, a house manager at a recovery program for women.

What Life Looks Like in Recovery

Recovery starts with structure. A day in a recovery program is less about perfection and more about consistency. There is an understanding that showing up on time and being prepared is part of rebuilding trust, both with others and with oneself. Planning and punctuality are a must, so we wake up on time, get to work on time, and show up to church on time.

Each day, the women wake up early, make their beds, and start their morning with intention. Before the responsibilities of the day begin, there is time set aside for devotions, prayer, and discussion. Living together and walking the road to recovery together builds a bond among the women. They get up together, pray together, cry together, study together, worship together, and often work a job together.

As the morning progresses, some residents go to work. Those who are just beginning their recovery journey stay in the house for the first few weeks, getting settled physically, mentally, and spiritually into the routine of the program.

Throughout the day, there are responsibilities that reinforce discipline and community. Outside of working their 40-hours-a-week job, there are chores to complete. The house is cared for and kept clean and orderly, and everyone contributes. The chore schedule on the wall shows each woman that she is part of a team, and as such she carries her portion of the responsibility. Whether it's cleaning, cooking, or taking out the trash, everyone pitches in, all the way down to who makes the coffee in the morning. These simple tasks restore dignity and remind residents that they are capable of maintaining a healthy, stable life.

Fostering a healthy and stable environment is essential for resident growth and recovery. Teaching life and coping skills, as well as addressing past trauma through various curricula, gives them the tools they need to live a life of sobriety outside the program. The residents also give back and rediscover a sense of value and connection through community outreach and service.

As the day begins to slow down, stories are shared, victories are celebrated, and struggles are acknowledged without judgment. We gently remind each other that no one is doing this alone. There is comfort in routine, safety in structure, and hope in knowing that each day lived sober is a step forward.

Life in a recovery program is not easy, but it is intentional. It's a daily commitment to healing, accountability, faith, and community, one day at a time.

What you'll notice in these daily rhythms is that none of them are extreme. They're simple, repeatable practices that mirror what healthy Christian living is supposed to look like all along. Faith-based recovery doesn't create an artificial bubble. It rehearses real life in a safer environment.

That's why it prepares people not just to graduate, but to reenter the world with tools, habits, and expectations already in place. When done right, recovery doesn't produce dependency on a program. It produces men and women who know how to live, serve, and stay connected long after the structure is gone.

When Healing Comes Full Circle

I think back often to Susan, the mother whose story I told in chapter 1. She once sat across from me and asked a question no parent ever wants to ask. She wanted to know if it was okay to stop rescuing her son, to release him from her hands and place him fully into God's. She loved her son so much, but that love had been exhausted by fear and heartbreak.

She prayed, "Lord, take my child from my hands into Yours."

That surrender felt like loss at the time, but it turned out to be the beginning of restoration. The son she thought she might lose forever did come back.

Today, the relationships in her family that once felt fractured beyond repair have been restored. Her son is present again both physically and emotionally. He's sitting at Christmas dinners, engaging with family, showing up in ways that addiction never allowed. Photos of him a year apart tell the story. Before going to faith-based recovery, there's a photo of him at Christmastime with his young niece sitting on his knee. His eyes are dull, and he's not interacting with her at all. You can tell he's disengaged.

But this past Christmas, things were different. I saw a photo of him with the same niece. Only this time, they're interacting face-to-face, and you can see the love and connection between them.

Punishment couldn't bring that son home. Grace did.

Passing Hope On

There's a simple truth that shows up again and again when healing is real. Healed people don't keep it to themselves. When someone has been rescued, something inside them changes. Gratitude turns into responsibility, and freedom creates a pull toward others who are still trapped.

That's why recovery, when it's rooted in grace, becomes living proof of the gospel's power. "If He did it for me, He'll do it for you" is a powerful testimony that carries a weight no policy, program, or punishment ever could.

This is where the work begins to move inward. Breaking cycles doesn't start with systems or institutions. It starts with individuals who decide to live differently. It starts with men and women who take responsibility for their own healing and then step into the role of becoming part of the solution.

What comes next is about that responsibility. About the daily choices that keep healing intact and people who refuse to pass pain forward and choose instead to pass hope on.

CHAPTER 13

Either You Break It or
You Pass It Down

I sat across from a woman at a small table in a quiet room. She'd already lost almost everything, including most of her relationships, trust, health, and even her freedom. Surprisingly, what's left in her isn't anger. It's resignation. You can see it in the way she hangs her head, not looking me in the eye. She's made peace with the idea that this is just who she is now. She's an addict. She can't change.

At that moment, I knew that using logic to appeal to her wasn't going to work. Neither would making threats about longer jail sentences or painting a picture full of hope for the future. Her unspoken belief sits between us, simple and devastating: *I'm not worth the effort.*

Somewhere along the way, shame convinced her that rescue was for other people who hadn't failed as badly as she had. If I stood a chance of convincing her to get help, I had to appeal to something—or someone—else.

"If you won't do this for yourself, would you do it for your children?"

Her head tilts up, and she looks at me for the first time. She loves her children, so I have her attention now. Good.

"Because if you don't break this addiction," I say carefully yet honestly, "they will have to."

That's when the tide turns for her, and a spark comes back into her eyes. Because even when a person has given up on themselves, they often haven't given up on the next generation. In that space between despair and love, something shifts. It's not motivation yet. It's responsibility. Sometimes, that's the first crack where healing can finally begin.

But she has a really long way to go.

How People Get This Low

People don't wake up one day and decide they're worthless. That belief is learned over time, shaped by trauma, failure, and rejection. They internalize repeated messages, both spoken and unspoken, that tell them they don't measure up and never will. And addiction feeds on it.

Trauma and addiction strip away a person's identity long before they start self-destructing. When someone is reduced to a charge number, a diagnosis, or a problem to be managed, it becomes easier for them to stop seeing themselves as fully human. Society pulls away first. Then family and friends grow tired. Eventually, the person removes themselves from society before anyone else can.

Punishment reinforces this erosion when it's applied without restoration. Consequences are necessary, but when they're all a person ever receives, they start to believe pain is what they deserve. Shame settles in, and hope feels unrealistic, and even dangerous, because hoping means risking disappointment again.

Over time, people stop fighting not because they don't care, but because caring hurts too much. When someone reaches this place, recovery doesn't feel like redemption—it feels like something meant for other people. That's how a person gets low enough to believe they should disappear by separating from society, or worse, instead of being healed.

The Question That Breaks Through

When someone reaches the place where they no longer believe they are worth saving, you can't argue them out of it. Logic bounces off shame, and encouragement often sounds like noise. At that point, the only thing left that still has weight is love for someone else.

That's why I ask "Would you do it for someone you love?" It could be their child or a grandchild, niece, or nephew. Almost everyone has someone they care about who's coming behind them and watching how their life is playing out. This idea of "If you don't break it, you'll pass it down" hurts, but it's true, and it redirects their focus to responsibility.

Most people struggling with addiction didn't choose to start the fire they're standing in. But they do get to choose whether it keeps spreading. When the lens shifts from self-rescue to protecting the next generation, recovery stops feeling selfish and starts feeling necessary. If they're willing to stand between the fire and someone innocent, that can be enough to take the first step forward.

Becoming the Hero of the Story

Most people trapped in addiction don't see themselves as villains. They see themselves as the damage left behind after everything went wrong. But every story reaches a moment where someone has to decide whether the pattern continues or stops here.

Becoming the hero of the story doesn't mean being perfect or fearless. It means being willing to stand in the middle of the mess and say, "This ends with me." Because of their love for someone else, they can choose not to let addiction keep burning through the people who come after them. Whether it's a child who deserves a different future or a family member who shouldn't have to carry the same weight, from this new perspective, recovery stops being about self-improvement and becomes an act of protection.

Heroes don't erase the past, but they can interrupt it. They can step between the fire and the innocent, knowing the cost, and choose responsibility anyway. That choice is often the first real act of healing.

From the Addict to the Reader

Up to this point, it might feel like this chapter has been aimed at someone else. Someone with addiction who's hit bottom and needs to make a dramatic life change. But the truth is, this chapter doesn't belong to just one group of people.

The same choice shows up in families, churches, and communities. You may not personally struggle with addiction, but you can still help fight addiction for the next generation. If you won't step in because it's uncomfortable or inconvenient, addiction gets passed down.

Every reader has a role in this story. Some have influence. Others have resources. Still others have proximity to those with addiction. Caring about this issue is a good start, but it's not enough to just say we care. We have to step forward and take action. We need to turn the mirror around and ask ourselves, "Will I get involved to save the next generation?"

If not now, when?

If not your church, then whose?

If we don't step into this gap and each do what we can, the next generation will be the ones who pay the price.

Proof That Legacy Can Change

I've seen what happens when someone decides to break the cycle instead of surrendering to it. The stories don't all look the same, but they carry the same quiet power and offer proof that legacy is not fixed. It was Christmastime as I wrote this book, and I saw an amazing example of a changed legacy in Vickie's story.

Vickie's story is one of those that reminds you how wide the damage can spread when addiction takes root and how far healing can reach when it's finally interrupted.

By the time I met Vickie, addiction had already woven itself through multiple layers of her family. This wasn't just about one woman struggling. It was about relationships that had been bent and broken over years. Vickie carried pain from her own past and suffered from wounds that were never addressed and losses that never had time to heal. Drugs didn't create that pain, but they gave it somewhere to hide for a while.

As her addiction deepened, the roles inside her family began to reverse. Responsibilities shifted in unhealthy ways. Her 11-year-old daughter carried emotional weight no child should ever have to bear. Instead of a carefree childhood, she had to grow up too fast, and she was always worrying and on guard. Her mother was present, but not fully available.

Holidays made that reality impossible to ignore. For every Christmas her daughter could remember, Vickie had spent the day in the car getting high instead of in the house with the family. Eventually, Vickie reached a point where the cycle could no longer continue. She asked for help and faced the damage she'd done honestly. She went into recovery, and her daughter went to live with her grandmother for a time.

While in treatment, Vickie was forced to look at herself without numbing, to sit with the consequences of her choices, and to take responsibility without being crushed by shame. Healing didn't happen all at once. It came in stages. Slowly, something remarkable began to take shape. Relationships started to stabilize, and trust was rebuilt through consistency. Vickie, her mother, and her sister reconciled and began coming to visit on family days.

But the most powerful change showed up in her daughter. The child who once lived on edge began to relax. The burden lifted. She could laugh and be a kid again. Every visiting day, you could find Vickie and her daughter seated close together, side by side. Healing moved beyond the individual and into the next generation.

Right after Christmas, I ran into Vickie's daughter. She was glowing as she excitedly said, "Pastor Brett! I got to spend all day at Christmas with my mom! She didn't stay in the car this time!"

Today, Vickie's story stands as proof that legacy doesn't have to repeat itself. Addiction had written one version of her family's future, but it wasn't the final draft. When Vickie chose recovery, she didn't just change her own life. She altered the trajectory of everyone who came after her. She gave her child back her childhood.

That's what breaking the cycle looks like.

Insights for Parents and Families

Loving someone with addiction is one of the hardest things a family can do. As mentioned earlier in this book, the go-to instincts we use to protect us, like rushing to the rescue, covering things up, and smoothing things over, can become the very things that interfere with breaking the cycle. Most parents and families don't enable because they're careless. They enable because they're desperate to keep someone alive.

One of the hardest lessons families have to learn is that love and boundaries are not opposites. Loving well often means allowing consequences to land while staying emotionally present. It means saying, "I won't abandon you—but I won't protect the addiction either."

Letting go is not the same as giving up. Surrendering someone into God's care doesn't mean stepping away in indifference. It means recognizing where your control ends and His begins. That kind of surrender takes courage, faith, and support, especially when fear has been running the show for a long time.

Families also need community. Addiction isolates not just the person using, but everyone who loves them. Trauma-informed support, trusted counsel, and a church that understands both grace and boundaries can make the difference between a family collapsing under the weight and one that learns how to stand together again.

Healing in families is rarely fast, but it is possible. When parents and loved ones learn how to love without enabling and to trust God with outcomes they can't control, they stop passing pain forward and start passing strength instead.

The Line in the Sand

There comes a moment when neutrality stops being an option. When seeing the damage, the pain, and the cycles repeating in front of you forces you to decide whether you'll keep looking away or step into helping people heal. That moment is the line in the sand.

Don't wait to cross that line until you have all the answers. Cross it because doing nothing has finally become unacceptable. Cross it because passing the problem down feels heavier than taking responsibility now. Cross it because you've realized that silence, however unintentional, still leaves people alone in their suffering.

Drawing a line in the sand doesn't mean you'll never fail or feel afraid. It means you've decided that indifference and neutrality are no longer on the table. Every life changed begins with someone who refused to stay neutral, stepped over the line, stood their ground, and chose to act.

What Can I Do?

One of the most common responses I hear from well-intentioned people is "I don't know enough to help." It sounds like a humble statement. More often than not, it becomes a reason to stay on the sidelines. The truth is, you don't need a degree, a title, or a perfect plan to help someone with addiction. All you need is willingness.

Everyone has something to offer. Like I said earlier in the chapter, some people have influence, others have time, resources, or proximity to someone who is hurting. Others have a voice that, when used at the right moment, can change the direction of a life.

The first step is almost always advocacy. Speak up when it would be easier to stay quiet. Ask a question, make a phone call, or stand with someone who feels invisible. Small acts of courage often open doors that policies and programs never could.

You don't have to fix everything. You just have to do *something*. Because when enough people decide to stop waiting for permission and start stepping forward, responsibility begins to replace resignation, and things begin to change.

In the next chapter, I'm going to get very specific about what it looks like to step into those roles. I'm going to break down specific ideas and suggestions for how you can get involved in your community in a way that can create a positive ripple effect that spreads. If you've been wondering, "What can *I* do?", the next chapter is for you.

CHAPTER 14

You Are the Solution

Jonah was a prophet, so it was his job to listen to God and relay what He said to others. Pretty straightforward. Except this time, Jonah was almost certain he must have misunderstood.

"Lord, surely not," said the prophet, turning his face toward heaven. "Surely you don't want me to go to Ninevah." But if Jonah was hoping for a different answer, he didn't get it.

"Get up," replied God. "I want you to go to Nineveh and tell them that unless they repent, I'm going to destroy their city."

Actually, the destruction of Nineveh didn't sound like such a bad idea to Jonah. The Ninevites were known to be awful, wicked people. Why would God want to give them a second chance? In Jonah's eyes, they didn't deserve God's mercy.

So Jonah got on a ship. But instead of obeying God and heading to Nineveh, he tried to run from God's presence and set sail in the opposite direction. Here's the thing you need to understand: Jonah didn't run because he didn't know God. He ran because he knew exactly what God would do, and he didn't like it.

And if you've ever heard the story of Jonah, you know that didn't turn out too well for him.

Because Jonah was not, in fact, able to hide from God. God sent a fierce storm, and Jonah was thrown overboard into the sea in order to save the rest of the ship's passengers. He ended up inside the belly of a big fish for three days and three nights, where he had plenty of time to think about how foolish it had been to run from God. When God caused the fish to vomit Jonah back up on shore, He only had one instruction for His prophet—go to Nineveh.

This time, Jonah went, but he wasn't happy about it. He still didn't think the Ninevites deserved to be saved. He could tell God was serious about His instructions though—three days in the belly of a fish made that really clear. He decided he'd just go to Nineveh, do his duty, and leave.

It's not like the people of Nineveh are going to listen anyway, Jonah thought to himself. They're so wicked, they don't even believe in God. They won't care what He says. They'll never change, and they'll get what's coming to them.

Nineveh was a large city for its time. It took about three days to walk across it. When Jonah arrived at the edge of the city, he walked about one day's journey towards the center, chose a public location, and yelled, "In 40 days, God's going to destroy Ninevah!"

Then he turned around and walked right back out of Nineveh. He found a comfy place far enough away where he could watch the fallout, and he wasn't about to miss the show. He sat down and waited for God to destroy the city.

Except He didn't. Even though Jonah had been a very reluctant prophet and delivered God's message with the bare minimum effort, the people of Nineveh received it. They believed it. They repented with sackcloth and ashes, all the way up to the king of the city himself. They changed their ways, and God saw it all. He knew the change was real, so he had mercy on the city and spared it.

Meanwhile, outside the city, 40 days came and went, and… nothing. Jonah was stunned, then angry. He knew what had happened.

"How could you save those people, God?" He shouted at the sky. "This is why I didn't want to come here! I know that you're a good God who shows mercy and love. I knew if I came here that you'd spare them, but they don't deserve it. How could you?"

Jonah had already forgotten what it felt like to be in dire circumstances. He forgot the three days and nights he had spent in the belly of a fish, begging for God's mercy and grace, which God gave him. The same grace he had received, he wanted to withhold from others who weren't like him.

Turns out, sometimes the hardest part of obedience isn't sacrifice. Sometimes the hardest part is surrendering the right to decide who deserves grace. In this chapter, you'll learn how you can join the army we are raising and get involved with addiction recovery. But before we talk about how to get involved as individuals, we need to confront what so often stops people before they ever take the first step.

Scripture gives us a brutally honest picture of that resistance in the story of Jonah. His struggle wasn't ignorance, fear, or lack of calling. He was reluctant to care for people he didn't think deserved it. The real test of obedience is not whether we'll follow God, but whether we'll follow Him to places we don't like. If we're going to step into this work with open eyes and honest hearts, we have to start by deciding to care.

Decide to Care

Every real movement starts with a decision, not a plan. Before you sign up, show up, or figure out what to do next, take a quiet moment and settle something in your heart. You've reached the point where indifference is no longer an option. So even though it won't be convenient or comfortable, decide to care.

Caring is not a personality trait. It's not reserved for the soft-hearted or the naturally compassionate. Caring is a choice you make when you decide that what's happening around you matters enough to interrupt your life. Most people don't avoid helping because they're cruel. They avoid it because they've trained themselves not to feel.

Caring requires intention because once you start caring, things get personal. Names replace statistics, and stories replace stereotypes. When that happens, you can't unsee what you've seen or unknow what you now know.

Deciding to care doesn't mean you suddenly have answers. It just means you're willing to stop looking away. Once that decision is made, everything else, like learning, speaking, or showing up, has a foundation to lean on when things become challenging.

I don't know about you, but I don't want to be like Jonah, sitting outside the city throwing a temper tantrum. We can disagree with the lifestyle of addiction while still praying for and helping people recover.

Deciding to care is the turning point, but it's not the finish line. Once your heart is engaged, you have to decide what to do about it. Caring pulls you out of neutrality and places you at a crossroads where obedience begins to cost something. Because once you start to care, the next step is to start speaking up.

Silence Is Not Neutral

Silence always feels safer than speaking up. It lets you stay on the sidelines, helps you avoid conflict, and keeps your life orderly. But in moments of need, silence is a decision. When we choose not to engage, not to speak, and not to act, we're still choosing a side.

In the story of Jonah, silence looked like distance. He dropped his truth bomb and got right out of town. He didn't stick around to urge people to repent. He didn't argue or debate with the Ninevites. He simply removed himself and hoped the problem would take care of itself. That same impulse shows up today when we convince ourselves that addiction, brokenness, or injustice is someone else's responsibility.

The truth is, silence protects comfort, not people. It allows systems to continue unchecked and suffering to remain unseen. When those with influence, faith, or resources stay quiet, the people who pay the price are those who are already hurting.

Neutrality sounds reasonable, but it doesn't exist in real life. If we're silent in the face of need, the status quo wins. And in this fight, the status quo is already destroying lives. It's time to start speaking up.

Your Voice Matters

One of the easiest lies to believe is that your voice doesn't really count. You tell yourself that someone else is more qualified, more informed, more articulate, or better positioned to speak up, so you stay quiet. It's not because you don't care, but because you assume your contribution won't make a difference anyway. That's a lie.

God has never waited for perfect messengers. Jonah didn't deliver a polished sermon. He didn't organize a campaign or build relationships first. He simply opened his mouth and said what God told him to say, and God did the rest. The power was never in Jonah's eloquence. It was in his obedience, as reluctant as it was.

Your voice works the same way. It may sound small to you, but it carries weight in places no one else can reach. You have relationships, credibility, and access that others don't. When you speak up in a church meeting, a courtroom, a family conversation, or a community space, you give permission for others to stop pretending everything is fine. You give courage to those who've been afraid to speak up. You bring hope to someone who needs to know you care.

You don't have to have all the answers to use your voice. It doesn't have to be eloquent or dramatic. Most of the time, it's simply being willing to say what others are avoiding.

It's asking in a courtroom whether punishment is actually helping or just recycling someone through the same system.

It's calling a treatment center and saying, "I know his record, but I also know who he could become if someone gives him a chance."

It's speaking up inside the church and admitting, "We can't say we love the broken and then panic when they actually show up."

Sometimes it's sitting across from a family member and saying, "I love you too much to pretend this is normal," or looking at someone fresh out of addiction and telling them, "You're not a project. You belong here."

Every story of recovery I've ever been part of started the same way—someone chose to speak when silence would have been easier.

When You Don't Know What to Say

Most people hesitate to speak up because they think they need permission, training, or expertise. The truth is, all you really need is to be willing to start a conversation about addiction and recovery. If you're a sports fan who watched an incredible football game over the weekend, you don't need an invitation to talk about it. Overhearing someone two tables away mention the game is enough to get you to jump right into the conversation. There's instant common ground, and the conversation unfolds naturally because you already share something.

Speaking up for recovery works the same way. You don't have to force the topic. You look for people who are already connected to it, like parents, coworkers, church members, friends. People whose lives have been touched by addiction whether they talk about it openly or not are great people to start a conversation with. When you recognize the connection you share, you have a starting place.

You can even use this book to start a conversation. Saying, "I just read something that really opened my eyes," is often enough to begin. Stories create space. Testimonies invite dialogue. And the more you listen and share, the more comfortable you become.

Using your voice is where involvement begins, but it's not where it ends. Speaking up cracks the door open. It signals that you care. It shows that you see what's happening and are no longer willing to stay silent. But words alone don't carry people very far.

The next step is letting that voice turn into action. Advocacy is what happens when you move from saying, "This isn't right," to asking, "What can I do to help?" It's the shift from awareness to responsibility, from concern to commitment. Once you decide to speak, the natural question becomes whether you're willing to become an advocate and walk with someone long enough to help change the outcome.

Becoming an Advocate

Advocates are people who are willing to stand beside and speak up on behalf of someone who can't do it for themselves. Becoming an advocate doesn't require credentials, a title, or having all the answers. Most of the people I've seen rescued didn't need an expert. They needed someone willing to stay engaged with them when things got complicated.

You don't have to start in a jail or a recovery house. Most people don't. Start in conversations. Start in church hallways. Start with one person who already cares but doesn't know what to do next. Advocacy grows the same way fandom does—one connection at a time, spreading person to person—until you realize you're no longer just observing. You're involved.

Advocates aren't there to fix someone. They're there to help them get to the people and places that can. You would make a good advocate if you're willing to ask questions about things you don't fully understand yet, make phone calls you've never made before, and admit, "I don't know what to do next, but I'm not leaving."

The moment you decide you have to be an expert, you'll talk yourself out of getting involved. You'll wait until you think you're trained enough, confident enough, or informed enough. While you wait, people with addiction stay stuck. Instead, choose to move with humility, curiosity, and persistence, and trust that God will fill in the gaps you can't.

The truth is, experts often change systems, but advocates change outcomes. One steady voice, one consistent presence, one person willing to keep showing up can alter the trajectory of an entire life. And often, that's exactly how God chooses to work.

Practical Ways to Step In

Once you decide to care and begin using your voice to advocate for addiction recovery, I urge you to take the next step. Start showing up where recovery is already happening. Not sure where the recovery centers are in your area? Ask around. Call your pastor. Open your web browser and do a Google search for "recovery program near me." Pull up their websites and see if they have volunteer information online.

Below, I've outlined some of the most common ways to show up. There are plenty of options, and you should choose one that fits within your time and talents. Here are some ways you can get more involved.

Attend Events

One of the simplest ways to get involved is by attending events connected to recovery work. Many recovery programs hold fundraisers, benefit dinners, 5Ks, community gatherings, and awareness events throughout the year. You don't have to volunteer or speak. Just being present matters. These spaces help you learn the language, meet the people, and see the work up close without pressure.

Visit Recovery Spaces

If you're willing, step into recovery spaces themselves. Family Nights are open to the public in most recovery centers, and they are some of the most honest, welcoming rooms you'll ever enter. You're not expected to fix, preach, or advise. You're there to listen, learn, and treat people like people. The format is simple. Each family night usually includes

- music,
- group discussion and sharing time,
- a devotional, and
- food.

It means so much to someone who's struggled with addiction to see people showing up, starting conversations, and truly caring about them. Once you see the need up close, it's hard to walk away unchanged.

Behind-the-Scenes Support

Not all support has to be front-facing. Maybe you don't have much time, but you're willing to financially support your local recovery program. That's great! Many people underestimate how valuable steady, behind-the-scenes support really is. Recovery work doesn't just run on passion. It runs on the reliable support of people who care.

One-on-One Mentorship

If you're ready to take on a deeper role, there's a huge need for mentorship. When I say mentorship, I'm not talking about fixing someone's life or becoming their spiritual supervisor. At its core, mentorship is choosing to walk with one person at a steady pace through their recovery and beyond, even when things get uncomfortable. Most people in recovery don't need another expert. They just need consistency from someone who cares.

Good mentorship looks a lot like listening, showing up, asking honest questions, and letting trust build over time. It's more of a commitment than showing up to an event or family night. You will need to go through some training and learn how to set boundaries. There will be rules you'll need to follow, so don't be offended or surprised if you have to take a drug test.

It's all worth it, because mentorship also impacts both parties. I've watched mentors walk in thinking they were there to give, only to realize they were being shaped just as much in the process. Patience grows as compassion deepens, and suddenly their faith becomes less theoretical and more practiced.

Not all mentorship looks the same. There may be structured mentorship opportunities for specific topics, like building relationships, holding down a job, or managing finances. In a more general mentorship situation, organizations often have talking points you can follow. Don't get hung up on the details. The most important thing is just to be willing to be someone's friend.

One faithful relationship, handled with humility and care, can change the trajectory of a life. When done well, mentorship doesn't create dependence. When people feel seen and respected, they're far more willing to receive the kind of guidance that helps someone stand on their own and eventually walk alongside others.

Start With What You Have

One of the biggest misconceptions about getting involved is the idea that you need special skills or an abundance of time and resources. In reality, God almost always starts with what's already in your hands. Don't focus on what you think you lack. Look at what you already have that you're willing to offer. I promise, it's enough.

Some people have practical skills. They can drive, cook, fix things, organize, build, or create. Those things can be used to prepare a recovering person for reentry into society. Others have relational gifts, like the ability to listen, encourage, notice when someone is struggling, or make people feel welcome. Those things may not feel spiritual, but in recovery work, they're often the most powerful tools in the room.

I've also seen people use music, art, crafts, and trade skills as bridges into connection and healing. I've seen others simply provide transportation to recovery programs states away, help someone get to an appointment, or show up consistently so a person knows they're not forgotten.

God wastes nothing. Your wiring, your experiences, and even your past mistakes make you the perfect person to start offering what you already have.

One of the most appreciated things you could do is pick up the phone and call a recovery organization to ask, "How can I help?" Most recovery programs will be glad to answer any questions you have. The organization may have opportunities that fit you that I haven't mentioned here. Don't hesitate to ask what you can do. The possibilities are endless. Here are just a few of the ways people I know are involved in recovery ministry:

- A friend of mine doesn't feel comfortable mentoring, but he has a car and is willing to drive. He volunteers his time to drive people to treatment centers up to two states away.
- Another friend of mine owns a business that wraps vehicles professionally. He provides signage and decals for a local recovery program.
- A group of musicians from a local church attend family night and lead worship music.

If you think you have nothing to offer, you're wrong. Whatever it is you do, God can and will use it. Will you let Him?

The Final Decision

In Jonah's story, it was never really about Nineveh. It was about Jonah's heart. God had shown mercy, lives had been spared, and a city had turned, but Jonah sat outside the gates angry and convinced that grace had been wasted on the wrong people.

That same moment confronts us now. Once you see the need, once you hear the stories, once you understand what's possible, you don't get to pretend you didn't know. The decision isn't whether broken people deserve grace. The decision is whether we're willing to obey even when grace offends our sense of fairness.

God didn't just want Jonah to deliver a message. He wanted Jonah to reflect His heart. That's what he wants for us too. So, what will you do with what you've read in this book?

Will you sit outside the city and wait to see what happens?

Will you look down on people stuck in their trauma?

Or will you step into the story God is already writing and join the army we are building? Mercy is moving. Healing is happening. The invitation is standing right in front of you. There's no one-size-fits-all way to get involved.

The only thing left to decide is whether you're willing.

CONCLUSION

"So Jesus said to them again, 'Peace to you! As the Father has sent Me, I also send you,'" (John 20:21 NKJV).

As this book comes to an end, I want to leave you with a send off. We've walked through the justice system, families, churches, recovery programs, and individual hearts. We've talked about punishment, healing, trauma, grace, obedience, and surrender. But none of that matters if it doesn't move you.

When Jesus appeared to His disciples after the resurrection, they didn't have a strategy meeting or create a five-year plan. He simply spoke a sentence that changed everything:

"As the Father has sent Me, I also send you." (John 20:21)

Jesus knew what it felt like to be sent out. He himself was sent into brokenness. He stepped into leper colonies, tax collector homes, prison cells, and graveyards. He did not hover at a safe distance. He entered the mess and loved others. Then He looked at the ordinary men and women who followed Him and said, "Now you go."

That's the moment we're standing in. Because once you've seen what grace can do, once you've watched hollow eyes come back to life, once you understand that punishment alone cannot heal what's broken, you can't stay neutral. But before you go out, check the posture of your heart.

The Heart Issue Beneath the Surface

In the previous chapter, we talked a lot about Jonah's heart. Before you step into this work, be aware that one way or another, you'll deal with issues of the heart as well.

Sometimes you'll deal with your own heart issues. If we're honest, it's not easy working with people who are different than we are. Deep down, it's easy to hold a quiet resentment toward people who are down and out like addicts, the homeless, and people who just keep messing up.

Sometimes, you'll have to deal with other people's heart struggles because there are people even inside churches who struggle when ministries help "those people." There's an unspoken feeling that they don't deserve help. Maybe they should suffer a little more. The church or community's time and money should be spent on those who are more deserving.

Nobody complains when you help someone successful or resents it when you serve someone who "earned it." But when you go into the ditches and lift up the least of these, you will encounter Jonahs. Some of them may even be sitting in the pew next to you.

If you're not careful, you might be one of them.

Settle this matter in your heart before you walk into a ministry. Grace cannot be earned by any of us. None of us deserve it.

That's what Jesus was getting at in the story of the banquet that I told you in chapter 10. The ones who fed the hungry, clothed the naked, and visited the sick and imprisoned weren't doing it for applause or a reward. They didn't even realize they were serving the King. Their actions flowed from their hearts because that's just who they were.

Before you start or join a ministry, ask yourself the Jonah question: Am I willing to celebrate mercy—even when it lands on someone I wouldn't have chosen? If your heart is aligned with His, you'll rejoice when the most unlikely person is restored.

The Carrot and the Horse

There's another attitude of the heart we must be careful about, and it's illustrated perfectly in a story often attributed to Charles Spurgeon.

A gardener harvested the most beautiful carrot he had ever grown. He thought to himself, *My prince has been good to me. I love him. I'm going to give him this carrot simply because I want to.*

So he brought the beautiful carrot to the prince and placed it in his hands. The prince thanked him, and without expecting anything in return, the gardener turned to leave. The prince, seeing that the gift was given purely out of love and not ambition, called him back and said, "I'm going to give you some of my land so you can grow even more." And the prince did.

Word of this spread through the kingdom. A nobleman heard the story and thought, *If the prince gives land for a carrot, imagine what he would give for one of my finest horses.* So he brought the most magnificent horse from his stable and presented it before the prince.

The prince looked at him and said, "I know why you've brought this. You heard about the carrot. But these two gifts are not the same. When the gardener gave me a carrot, he gave it to *me*. When you gave me this horse, you gave it because of what you thought *you'd* get in return."

Ouch. It's easy to drift into doing good for what we'll get out of it. Recognition and applause are attractive. Doing something for others can come from a sense of moral superiority. But when we serve to be seen, we've already received our reward. That's not what we're talking about in this book.

Jonah struggled with this to the very end. He obeyed, but his heart lagged behind. He delivered the message, but he still sulked under the bush. He wasn't aligned with the mercy of God. He wrestled with it.

If we're going to step into the ditches, the trap houses, the jail pods, and the broken homes, we have to check our motives. Are we giving the carrot? Or are we giving for what we can get? This work isn't about being seen doing good things. It's about loving the King enough to serve the least of these, whether anyone ever notices or not.

Standing in the Gap With Deborah

Even if your heart is right, getting started in recovery ministry can still feel intimidating. You can love God and feel the call and still hesitate when it's time to move. You can agree with the mission and still feel unqualified to step into it. That tension isn't new.

In Judges 4 and 5, we meet Deborah. She was a prophetess and a judge in Israel, a woman who clearly heard from God and spoke His will. She was there and heard God when he called Barak, a male leader, to confront oppression and step into battle.

God made His will clear. Barak should go, gather the men, and move forward. But Barak hesitated. He said he would go, but only if Deborah went with him. His obedience came with conditions.

So Deborah went, and the mission moved forward. God's purposes were not stalled by Barak's hesitation, and the Israelites still won. But because he was reluctant, the honor of the final blow of the battle did not go to him. It went to someone else.

Barak's calling delayed became his calling displaced. That story should shake us a little.

God's plans are not fragile. He is not wringing His hands in heaven, hoping you cooperate. If He wants to raise up recovery ministries, restore families, and rescue people out of addiction, He will do it with or without you. The only question is whether you will be part of it.

God uses available people. Deborah didn't force herself into the story. She simply stood in the gap when someone else hesitated. She was willing, present, and obedient. Are you?

God's will is clear. We know people need help. We know addiction is ravaging families. We know the church is called to step in. So where is God asking you to step into the gap, and what's holding you back?

Are you waiting to "feel" ready? God's not looking for your preparedness. All God really wants is your obedience. Barak eventually moved, but the legacy shifted. God's call is not endangered by our hesitation, but our legacy might be.

You may not feel bold or equipped or certain. But the truth is, God is not searching for perfect people. He's searching for willing ones.

Opportunities are not random. They are invitations. This book may simply be information for some, but for others, it may be a calling. The question is not whether God will act. The battle wages on, and He will act. The question is whether you will answer. Don't miss your moment.

From Punishing Sin to Fighting for Souls

Remember those laminated obituaries I keep in my desk drawer? Each represents a story that ended too soon. That drawer is a reminder of what addiction does when it runs unchecked, and I never want to forget that. It fuels me to keep in the fight.

But those aren't the only memories I keep. I've stood waist-deep in water with men who once couldn't stand on their own two feet and baptized them. I've attended graduations, weddings, and other celebrations. I have held the newborn babies of young couples now happy and sober. I've seen hollow eyes become steady and watched sons return to mothers who had already started grieving them. I'll never forget watching families sit at Christmas tables together who once couldn't sit in the same room.

Punishment alone never produces that kind of transformation. Only grace can.

Healing is possible. Legacies can change. What once looked permanent is not as final as we think. When we move from simply punishing sin to fighting for souls, the story changes. I have seen it with my own eyes, and it all started with one simple prayer: "God, let me see them the way You see them."

When you pray that prayer, anger and frustration will begin to soften. The fear that kept you at a distance will shift. Your excuses will begin to weaken, and your compassion will grow.

You'll stop seeing "addicts" and start seeing sons and daughters. Statistics will be replaced by stories, and you'll stop measuring people by their worst decisions and start remembering what grace did in your own life.

That prayer changed me. It moved me from a posture of control to one of surrender. I stopped seeing punishment as the answer and realized real healing was the goal. I quit standing at a distance and started stepping into the gap.

If you are serious about being part of this fight, start there. I dare you to pray this prayer too, but be careful. It will change you.

And when it changes you, everything else begins to change with it.

Next Steps

If something in you has been stirred while reading this, don't ignore it.

For some of you, the next step is personal. Go back to chapter 14 and revisit the practical ways you can step in right where you are by using your voice, becoming an advocate, mentoring someone, and showing up in small but intentional ways. Not everyone is called to start something new. Many are called to faithfully serve in existing places.

Others among you—especially those of you who are pastors, elders, ministry leaders, and community leaders—this isn't just about individual involvement. Gather your leadership team, read this book, and talk honestly about it together. Decide whether your church is willing to step into the trenches. Begin assessing what training, structure, and strategy would be needed to build a sustainable ministry.

If your church is feeling the pull to step into this work, you don't have to figure it out alone. I've walked this road from the courtroom to the church pew, from crisis response to long-term recovery. I've seen what works and what doesn't, and I've walked with a number of churches as they launch recovery ministries.

If you'd like help getting started building a recovery ministry that's both compassionate and sustainable, I'm willing to come alongside you. The need is real. The harvest is ready. If your church is ready to join the fight, I'd be honored to help you start.

Don't let hesitation steal the moment. Don't sit under the bush and wait for someone else to go first. God's purposes will move forward. The only question left is whether you and your church will stand in the gap. For more information and to contact me about speaking to your church or group, visit https://BrettKnight.com/book.

ABOUT THE AUTHOR

B rett Knight has spent his life standing in courtrooms—but his true calling has always been standing in the gap for the broken.

Born in Kansas, raised in Illinois, and settled in Tennessee as a young adult, Brett grew up in a loving but poor home. Hard work was not optional. He worked three part-time jobs to put himself through college and later built a successful career in information technology before answering a long-delayed call to attend law school.

After graduating from Belmont University College of Law, Brett served as a criminal prosecutor for the State of Tennessee before transitioning into private practice, where he now serves as a criminal defense attorney and City Judge.

But it was through the stories behind the cases—the addiction, the trauma, the generational pain—that Brett discovered the deeper work he was meant to do. For years, he has walked closely with individuals battling drug and alcohol addiction, many of whom entered the justice system at their lowest point. Instead of seeing only charges and convictions, Brett sees sons, daughters, mothers, and fathers as people created in the image of God, often carrying wounds long before they ever picked up a substance.

As an ordained pastor in Tennessee, Brett invests heavily in recovery ministry. He works alongside faith-based programs, mentors men and women coming out of incarceration, and advocates for restoration over condemnation. He believes firmly that accountability and mercy are not opposites—and that real transformation happens when truth is paired with grace.

Together with his wife Donna, a microbiologist who manages major hospital laboratories, Brett dedicates much of his time to helping individuals rebuild their lives after addiction and trauma. Their shared mission is simple: No one is beyond redemption.

Through his podcast, public speaking, and daily work in both the legal and ministry worlds, Brett continues to champion one central message: You cannot punish the pain away—but you can heal it.

He and Donna live in Tennessee and remain deeply committed to serving their community and walking with others toward freedom.

ACKNOWLEDGMENTS

Although the space on this page would not give me the room I need to acknowledge all the people and organizations that have assisted me with the experiences and knowledge contained in my thoughts shared in this book, I would not be able to conclude without recognizing at least a few people.

To my wife, Donna Knight, who is my biggest fan and encourager.

To those who lifted me up to higher levels along the way and saw in me something I had not yet seen. Men like George Hopkins and Dr. Ron Mason and many others who showed up just at the right times in my life and spoke just the right words to propel me forward.

To all those who stand beside me in spiritual battles and serve with me in ministry. You answer calls at 2 a.m. and show up in desperate places to meet with desperate people. You stand in the gap and man the walls.

To my colleagues in the courtroom who fight every day to set just one more person free from addiction.

Finally, I want to acknowledge and cheer on those who have just recently accepted the call to arms—those of you who have read this book and are drawn to enlist. Know that your decision is already beginning to turn the tide of the battle. Your story, even unfinished, is the weapon.

"And they overcame him by the blood of the Lamb and by the word of their testimony..." (Rev 12:11 NKJV).